Every teen who self-injures needs to get this book into his or her hands. *Scars That Wound : Scars That Heal* is the compass needed to navigate the storm. And for those who are trying to help self-injuring teens, this book will finally answer your most important questions: Why do they do it? What can I do to help?

—Christian Hill, MA; Alpine Connection Counseling,
Colorado Springs

Scars That Wound : Scars That Heal is a powerful, gripping story marked with practical advice on how to escape the grip of self-injury. Anyone who is caught in its tangled web should read this. It could change their life!

—Megan Hutchinson, author of the eight-step recovery program
Life Hurts, GOD HEALS; Student ministries, Saddleback Church

Cutting . . . it's an ugly reality of life in today's world for far too many young adults, teens, and children. The cuts are cries for redemption and outward signs of that deep groaning for wholeness and healing. Jan takes readers on a difficult yet necessary journey into understanding cutting, but also shows the reader how to enter into that joyous journey that answers the groans.

—Dr. Walt Mueller, president, The Center for Parent/
Youth Understanding, Elizabethtown, Pennsylvania

Jan has written a sensitive approach to a subject more prevalent than most adults realize. Self-injury is driven by a massive amount of pain. This book offers hope and help through the real-life journey of one young hurting woman, and it doesn't pull punches. It reveals the hidden hurts of many of today's teenagers, using haunting images and stories that will stir your emotions, cause you to think, and at times make you cry. The book also offers strategies for responding to hurting teenagers. I highly recommend this book to students, parents, and youth leaders.

—Dr. Les Christie, chairman, youth ministry, William Jessup University; Youth Specialties Core Team

I just read this entire book, and it is incredible. I think everyone can see a bit of themselves in Jackie. Maybe they didn't hurt themselves by cutting or burning, but there are so many other ways that people don't even realize . . . So many times teens don't feel the love they've always craved from a parent, or perhaps they get involved with drugs or using their body as a toy instead of a temple. *Scars that Wound : Scars that Heal* goes places where other books can't.

For me, this book was so much more meaningful because it shared my pain of hurting myself, in words that I couldn't express. When Jackie had fights with her father, I couldn't help but think how that is an everyday battle for me, and for so many other kids. Like Jackie, I had no way of expressing my pain to others—besides cutting myself. I thought I was a failure and deserved pain because I was a terrible thing that needed more grace than Jesus could give, even when he died on the cross. I was once told, "There is nothing you could do to make God love you any less." This book has that statement written all over it, in many different ways, for many people to understand.

—Jessica, a former cutter

Scars That Wound : Scars That Heal breaks new ground in understanding the mind and heart of the self-injurer. Jan Kern has reached into the world of despairing kids with the hope of healing where there has been no hope. Each story compels the reader forward to grasp the deep realm of pain and loss that the self-injurer lives with. Then, at that lowest place, Jan leads us to Jesus—who is already there.

—Mike Petrillo, marriage and family therapist; executive director, Christian Encounter Ministries

I have worked with both young men and young women who self-injure through cutting, bone breaking, hair pulling, eating disorders, and substance abuse in outpatient services, in jails, and in prison. Jan reaches out to these hurting people with tenderness, love, and honesty. . . . *Scars That Wound : Scars That Heal* will help break the chains of your prison and lift you into the presence of God for healing, fullness of joy, and peace. If you know a self-injurer, Jan will help you understand and reach out with compassion and faith in the God who heals.

—Yvonne Ortega, LPC, LSATP, CCDVC; author, *Hope for the Journey Through Cancer: Inspiration for Each Day*

SCARS THAT WOUND : SCARS THAT HEAL

A JOURNEY OUT OF SELF-INJURY / / JAN KERN

A LIVE FREE BOOK

SCARS THAT WOUND : SCARS THAT HEAL

Standard
PUBLISHING
Bringing The Word to Life

Cincinnati, Ohio

Published by Standard Publishing, Cincinnati, Ohio
www.standardpub.com

Printed in the United States of America

Project editor: Robert Irvin
Cover design: Studio Gearbox
Interior design: Edward Willis Group, Inc.

Published in association with the Books & Such Literary Agency, 52 Mission Circle, Suite 122, PMB 170, Santa Rosa, CA 95409-5370, www.booksandsuch.biz.

ISBN 978-0-7847-2104-9

Library of Congress Cataloging-in-Publication Data

Kern, Jan, 1956-
 Scars that wound, scars that heal : a journey out of self-injury / Jan Kern.
   p. cm.
 ISBN 978-0-7847-2104-9 (perfect bound)
1. Christian teenagers--Religious life. 2. Self-mutilation—Religious aspects--Christianity. I. Title.

BV4531.3.K47 2007
248.8'627--dc22

2007000842

13 12 11 10 09 08 07   9 8 7 6 5 4 3 2 1

CONTENTS

ACKNOWLEDGMENTS

IN MANY WAYS, this book did not begin with me. All the stories were unfolding long before I became aware of them. Jackie's was the first I was privileged to hear. In God's scheme of things, a book was in the making. Somewhere along the way I figured out that I was supposed to go along for the adventure.

Jackie: you wanted to share your story and tears with me so others would know God's love in action. I know it wasn't easy. Thanks for catching me up in the ripples of his work in you. Can't wait to see where they go from here.

Jackie's family—Fred, Betty, and Nikki: your honesty in showing a family-in-progress was awesome. You are beautiful expressions of God's work in real people.

Jackie's friends and her spiritual family at Christian Encounter Ministries: you each said yes to God and made a difference.

All of you who shared your own journeys for this book: you put yourself out there, and that takes courage. You've been amazing.

Tom, my husband: when things get crazy, you come through.

My kids, Danny and Sarah: your phone calls and prayers mean the world to me.

Wendy, at Books & Such: you believed in this project from the start and have been not only a fantastic agent, but also a friend and support. I owe you a huge hug.

Bob Irvin and the staff at Standard Publishing: thanks for catching the vision for this book and making it happen. I prayed for the right publisher—and never wavered in the belief that I found it.

Many others joined in the adventure through prayer and encouragement. Thanks for helping me keep my eyes on Jesus Christ. He is the author and finisher of our faith, and in many ways, this book. Not a word of it could have been written without him.

FOREWORD

IF YOU ARE READING THIS BOOK because someone who cares about you asked you to, then trust that you have stumbled onto a very good thing. God is speaking to your heart. Read *Scars That Wound : Scars That Heal* with an open mind toward what he can do in your life. If you are self-injuring and feel that nobody understands why you do it, know that you are not alone—you're one of two million Americans who purposely self-injure. There are many others who experience a deep, immense pain that clouds their thoughts and makes them feel helpless. Allow this book to help you experience the journey toward healing and finding purpose in your life.

Or you may be reading this book because you know someone who self-injures. In either case, Jan Kern conveys a message of hope through the personal, true story of Jackie. Caught in the web of the painful memories of her past and overwhelming feelings of hopelessness, Jackie began to injure herself at the age of fourteen. She desperately wanted to tell those close to her how she felt, but couldn't do it with words. She believed the only way she could express the deep emotions that were building within her was through self-injury.

Have you ever felt like you just couldn't share your deepest feelings with another person? That no one would understand? That's how Jackie felt until she met someone who helped her find the source of her hurt. Healing requires making a personal commitment to positive action. First, make the simple, but profoundly important, decision that you want to heal. Second, consider if you should seek professional help from a therapist who specializes in these issues. Third, find caring people who will support you through the healing process. Finally, but most importantly, understand how much Jesus loves you and wants you to follow his plan for your life. If you take these steps, you'll be well on your way to recovery. But just as Jackie had setbacks, which you'll read about, don't expect things to change overnight. Healing from years of hurt and emotional pain will take time and patience.

Healing is never an easy journey. But it is one well worth the effort. With this book, Jan does a wonderful job of casting a vision of hope and healing for those who can't see a way out. If you're thinking you can never heal from the pain you have experienced, please consider this: picture a difficulty you had in your past that you eventually overcame. Did you doubt you could survive the ordeal? It may have been the death of someone close, a traumatic event in your family, moving to a new school, your parents' divorce, a suicide, or something else extremely difficult. How did you get through it? Perhaps without even knowing it, you used your personal strengths. I believe those strengths have always been there, that they are given to you at birth. Think of how they helped you through past challenges. Now think of how you can use those same personal strengths to help you through your present situation.

Maybe you also had the support of others to help you through your difficulty; everyone needs that type of encouragement. Getting involved with positive peer groups can help you take that step. Have you ever helped another person, volunteered at a homeless shelter or animal shelter, or helped a hurt or abandoned dog or cat? How did it feel? Using your

God-given gifts to help others is the greatest gift you can give yourself. When you reach out to others who are hurting, you find a sense of purpose in your life.

You can start today by sharing your pain with a caring, trustworthy friend. This book will help greatly. As you take the steps toward healing, God will reveal his plan for your life. His Son is the one who said, "With God all things are possible."

—Susan Bowman, EdS, LPC; author,
See My Pain and *Co-Piloting*

A BEGINNING . . .

You've picked up this book, so you probably have self-injured or you know someone who does. You're not alone. Many have turned to hurting themselves in some way in order to deal with the hard stuff in their lives.

If you self-injure, I hope that in these pages you'll discover—especially through Jackie's true story told here—how much God wants to be involved in your unique story. A story in which you can begin to head in a new direction out of self-injury and closer toward him.

Your reasons for wanting to hurt yourself and the pain and history behind it matter. Don't believe for an instant that no one would possibly care. God does, and he will help you find others who care too.

I don't consider this a self-help book because you can't tackle this alone. It's important you share what's going on with someone you can trust—and especially that you pray to God about what you're feeling. He'll show you more about his love for you and provide ways for you to stop hurting yourself. If you need to, don't hesitate to ask someone to help you find a Christian group, or a church, or a person you can go to for more support. Some resources are listed in the back of this book.

If you don't self-injure but know someone who does, the best way you can help him or her is to pray and be a friend. You may often feel you don't understand the reasons behind self-injury or exactly how to help. But God can use you and your love and patience as you simply listen or offer encouragement in handling the emotions, memories, and stresses differently.

I live and work at a ministry where teens come for help. It was at this place that I met Jackie, when she was eighteen, and we grew to be good friends. She wanted me to tell her story so that you would know that God is bigger than self-injury, anxieties, and fears. Through her story you'll see that in Jesus Christ you can find hope and know you are not alone.

Jackie shared her story with me through hours of conversation and through her blood- and tear-stained journals. In relaying it, she chose not to reveal the names or relationships of those who had molested her. Every attempt has been made to relay the events in Jackie's life as accurately as memories would allow. Real names were used, except for the teens in her youth group.

In the midst of all of Jackie's pain, what stood out most—as we looked back through those days—was how powerfully God worked through people he brought into her life. Even when responses and actions weren't perfect, every relationship brought about a little more healing and a little more revelation of the depth of the love and healing God had for Jackie.

In the second half of each chapter, following Jackie's story, you'll find a commentary section that includes stories from others who have taken similar journeys and are discovering the possibilities God has for their healing. In most cases, the names of the individuals who shared their stories have been changed.

I chose not to list many details about how a person self-injures, but in some cases mentioning some of them has to be part of the story. If you think you may come across personal triggers that make you want to hurt yourself, please read this book with someone instead of by yourself. It might be a good idea anyway—just to have someone to talk with and pray along with you.

Wherever you are on your journey, I want to encourage you to never give up. God will never give up on you. If you haven't already, begin to pray to him every day. Here's a prayer you can use if you'd like:

God, I hurt inside so much and it shows on the outside with all the scars and marks I've made. I want to stop believing that I deserve the pain I'm feeling and that everything is out of control. Instead, help me each day to begin to believe that I'm your child and you love me more than I can ever imagine. Help me with the pain that overwhelms me with sadness, anxiety, or fear. Each day may I grow closer to freedom from the desire to hurt myself. Today, as I lift my head up from prayer, I will try to keep my focus on you. If I fail a little, or even a lot, I won't be afraid to pray again tomorrow. AMEN.

I pray for new beginnings for you.

Jan

one

I always feel like I did something to deserve this.
I just want to know when it's going to be over.

—Jackie's Journal

Jackie clutched the tear-soaked covers surrounding her as she lay in her bed. Part of her wanted to burrow deeper into the blankets; part of her wanted to run. But where would she go at 11:00 at night?

I want a cigarette. Jackie slipped out of the covers, rolled off the bed, and rummaged through the piles on the floor, but only found a lighter. Gripping it tightly, she slammed her fist into her mattress. A new surge of tears racked her body and she slumped to the edge of her bed. *Why is everything so hard?*

Jackie rolled the lighter around in her hand. Her thumb slid down the lighter wheel and squeezed the tab. The flame erupted for a moment before she let it die. Several times she flicked and released the lighter. Each flame surge illuminated her dark, cramped bedroom. A flash: she saw clothes scattered across the floor. Another: pictures of family and friends on the wall and posters of music idols. Still another: two doors.

Jackie's room was a walk-through, meant to be an office. This year, at fourteen, she had moved out of the bedroom she shared with her younger sister. She liked having her own room. Even this small one. Besides, it had a straight shot to the back door—a great way to escape the tension at home.

She flicked on the lighter again. Jackie took several shaky breaths and her tears gradually slowed. Lately she felt upset all the time. *Why?* She released the lighter tab. The room went dark.

Dad had come home irritated about something—as usual. His stomping around sent her fleeing to her room. She was tired of his yelling and making her feel stupid. Tired of his smoking pot and drinking. Tired of seeing Mom look so sad and worn out. And there was something more—something she couldn't identify.

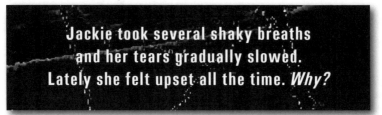

Jackie took several shaky breaths and her tears gradually slowed. Lately she felt upset all the time. *Why?*

She wiped her eyes.

Another press of her thumb and the lighter's flame shot up, illuminating her room again. She glanced down at the strewn clothes.

They reminded her of the day just after Christmas when she started cleaning her room. She accidentally stepped on a Christmas ornament, shattering it. As she cleaned up the sharp pieces, she thought of an article she'd read in a teen magazine— a story about a girl who had hurt herself to deal with her intense emotions. Jackie had never heard of people who intentionally cut or burned themselves. She had picked up a piece of the broken ornament and scratched a line across her arm—just to feel what it was like. Her skin welted as if scratched by a kitten, but it didn't hurt much or bleed.

Jackie let the lighter flame go out, then immediately made it flash again. Could she ever scratch deeply enough to bleed? Could she ever burn herself? Maybe—if she got mad enough.

She was getting pretty mad right then. Yeah, her dad frustrated her, but there was more to it. She'd been angry for weeks ... months ... maybe years. A couple years ago, her mom had become worried enough that one night she dropped Jackie off at a church youth group meeting. It was fun hanging out there, and she continued going, but it didn't help. The anger only grew. Especially after she saw the other kids who seemed to have perfect families.

Why is my family so messed up? Why am I so messed up?

The tears started again and she watched the lighter flame blur. She closed her eyes and swallowed. The anger grew more intense. She felt an awful pain inside that she couldn't name. It surged from deep inside her gut and threatened to grab her and hold her down. Fear flooded through her and her eyes shot open. She wanted to run. Her breathing quickened and her heart pounded. How could she make the feelings stop?

Could she ever scratch deeply enough to bleed? Could she ever burn herself? Maybe—if she got mad enough.

The lighter.

She tilted the flame to heat the top metal edge of the lighter and then pressed the hot part against her wrist. It hurt and she gasped, but the panic eased and the anger began to cool. She burned herself again. And then again. All the unwanted emotions seemed to slip away. Dad didn't matter anymore. The horrible fear was gone. She relaxed.

Jackie sat in the dark for a few moments before she reached over and flipped on the light switch. U-shaped marks covered her arms. She counted them. In just five minutes she had inflicted twenty-one burns.

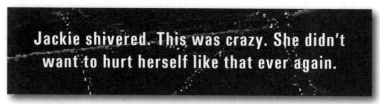

Jackie shivered. This was crazy. She didn't want to hurt herself like that ever again.

As the burns began to blister, they seeped and stung like fire. She knew she should take care of them, but how? Leaving her room wasn't an option. The last thing she needed was to wake up her parents. She grabbed tissues, pressed them over the burns, and climbed back under her covers. The burns hurt, but she preferred this pain over a surge of emotions she couldn't control.

What have I done?

Burning had eased the out-of-control feelings, but she'd only meant to try it once. When it calmed her, she thought she had pressed the lighter against her arm only a few more times. How'd she lose track?

Jackie shivered. This was crazy. She didn't want to hurt herself like that ever again. How would she handle these feelings the next time? She wanted to talk to someone—anyone but her parents. They'd only be mad. No way could they find out. She'd hide the burns. Maybe tomorrow at the youth breakfast she could talk to one of the leaders.

The next morning, a Saturday, Jackie and her dad acted as if

SCARS THAT WOUND : SCARS THAT HEAL

nothing had happened between them. *Typical for our family*, she thought. She tugged at her long sleeves to make sure they hid the reddened blisters. Avoiding any conversation, she headed to church for the breakfast.

While Jackie helped serve pancakes, she watched for a chance to talk to one of the youth sponsors. Finally, she served the last person. Crossing the room, she spotted Debbie and asked her if they could talk. They stepped outside, to the backyard of the church, and found a bench to sit on.

At first Jackie couldn't say anything, but Debbie was like a second mom to her. She'd care, no matter what. Slowly, haltingly, the words came. After Jackie explained that she had burned herself, she pulled up her sleeves to reveal the fresh burns. They still stung. Just as fresh was the memory of feeling out of control.

"I was going to burn myself only once, but I was mad and scared and I . . . I kept going."

Debbie squeezed Jackie's hand. "What made you so mad?"

"Dad. Stuff. I don't know." Tears pooled in her eyes. Nothing made sense, so how could she explain? What Dad did shouldn't have made her so mad that she'd hurt herself. "I don't know," she repeated.

"You've got a lot going on inside." Debbie brushed a tear that slipped down Jackie's cheek. "I think you should tell Melody. You've been talking to her a lot. She'd want to know."

"OK, I will," Jackie promised. Melody was the youth pastor and a special friend to Jackie. She would try to talk to her soon.

The next morning Jackie sat next to Melody during the

church service. Partway through the worship, she caught Melody's attention. Jackie lifted her sleeve to show her burns and watched as tears came to Melody's eyes. Gently, her youth pastor placed her hand over Jackie's blisters.

> Jackie watched her parents' expressions.
> They looked confused and already angry.
> This wasn't going to be easy.

After the service Melody turned to Jackie. "Your mom and dad need to know about this."

"I can't tell them."

"They need to know."

"I . . . I just can't."

"I'll call them, OK? We'll have a meeting here at the church—just me, you, and your parents."

Great. It wasn't so bad telling Debbie and Melody, but her parents would be furious. They liked to keep family stuff private. In the past when she said anything, she got in trouble. Her stomach knotted. *Is there any way out of this?*

The meeting time came too quickly. As everyone filed into Melody's office, Jackie watched her parents' expressions. They looked confused and already angry. This wasn't going to be easy.

They were a Hispanic family, their complexions golden brown. As they sat down, Mom's dark, natural curls fell forward and framed her concerned face. Dad leaned back, resting his hands on his thighs. At five-foot-four, Jackie was almost as tall as he was. Still, with his stocky build he was an intimidating man.

Melody began. "This morning Jackie told me something that you should know. The other night she was upset. She burned her arms." Melody turned to Jackie. "Can you show them?"

Jackie slumped in her chair and twisted her long hair around a finger. She wished she'd never shown anyone. Slowly, she lifted each sleeve. Her parents stared.

"Those are *burns*?" Dad leaned forward.

"Why would you do that?" Mom demanded.

Jackie jerked her sleeves back down. "I don't know." Her eyes filled with tears.

"You don't just go and burn yourself," Dad said, his voice rising. "What were you thinking?"

"I don't know. I was just mad."

"You were *mad*?" Dad said. "That's no reason."

Words wouldn't come. Jackie was left only with her thoughts. *Oh Dad, you don't understand. I don't even understand. Nothing I could say would make a difference. It wouldn't make you care. It wouldn't make the hurt inside go away. It wouldn't change anything.*

She pressed her hand over the burns. Even through the sleeves, they stung. She longed for the escape the pain had brought a few nights before.

Her parents' voices seemed far away. Jackie stopped trying to explain and sat and stared at nothing. She had shut down.

> **I have loved you with an everlasting love;**
> **therefore I have drawn you with lovingkindness.**
>
> JEREMIAH 31:3

"Why?"

When Jackie's parents asked her that question, they didn't realize how much it demanded. Her honest response—"I don't know. I was just mad"—was as much as she could risk. One more word, one more feeling would force her to go to places inside she didn't understand—places she wanted to avoid. She'd have to think through confusing emotions or recall frightening pieces of memories. *Not yet; it's not safe* is what her mind screamed if anyone—herself included—asked why.

At fourteen, Jackie didn't connect a lot of what had happened in her life with those moments when she felt out of control. She punched walls, slammed doors, or threw things across her bedroom. Then the day came when she burned herself for the first time. "I was always overwhelmed with emotions and didn't know what to do. I felt angry, anxious, and afraid," Jackie said as she looked back on those pain-filled years. "Little things set me off in a big way."

Her intense emotions pointed partly toward home. For Jackie, home wasn't a great place to be. Mom and Dad didn't get along. Dad was often angry and struggled with alcohol and drug abuse. Mom frequently threatened to leave. Jackie's biggest fear was that her mom would pack her bags and take off.

Though she knew her family struggled, she did everything she could to avoid blaming them. "I thought I was supposed to be responsible for the whole family," she shared later. "Even if my parents had a little fight, I thought I had failed to keep the family together. I worried about their finances and taking care of my younger sister, Nikki."

They didn't ask her to take on that responsibility; she just did. Her parents had worked since she was born. Though they naturally expected her to help out at home and with her younger sister, she took on much more. "I wanted to please them," Jackie admitted.

Those were the problems she could identify in junior high. And yet there were many more. Some childhood memories, too painful to describe or even to acknowledge, she tucked deep inside. Those would surface later, but they were a big part of the emotions behind the moment she burned herself twenty-one times.

After the meeting with Melody and her parents, Jackie's life spun quickly downhill. It no longer mattered if she understood her emotions. She'd cope with them through burning herself, drinking, taking drugs—whatever it took. She burned herself more often and began to cut herself. Her parents and the youth workers didn't question her about it because she fooled everyone into thinking she had hurt herself only once. She hid the burns and cuts under long, dark shirts and pants.

A couple years would pass before she would tell anyone about her secret self-injury. It would be even longer before she understood the deeper reasons she did it. At fourteen she had discovered only that the pain helped her calm down, and for a while that was reason enough.

In her newness to the Christian faith and her church, Jackie didn't realize that God could help her. In her eyes, he didn't care how she was doing. She believed he didn't like her and had plenty of reasons not to.

one

The journey ahead would prove to be long and difficult, but Jackie would learn that God loved her. He would gradually fill her heart with hope and bring people she could trust. As much as she initially tried, she wouldn't travel this road alone.

> The most common types of self-harming behavior are cutting and burning. Others include self-hitting, bone breaking, hair pulling, scratching, and interfering with the healing of wounds, such as picking at scabs. Self-injury can include any purposeful choice to harm oneself.

YOUR OWN REASONS

Does this story sound familiar?

Self-injury—the deliberate choice to habitually harm yourself—doesn't happen without reason. For some of you, it's the only way you can express and cope with the hurt, anxiety, anger, or fear you feel. Even if you don't understand it all yet, you have reasons that you hurt yourself—painful reasons trapped inside with seemingly no place to go. By your own hand you've brought your inside pain to the outside. You see it now in the scars left from the injuries you've inflicted on yourself.

You're not alone. Just like Jackie and just like you, others have faced unexpected, intense situations that blasted them with emotions they didn't know how to handle.

"I felt controlled by everyone in my life—my parents, my pastor, even my friends," one said.

This is what others said:

"My mom's boyfriend molested me."

"My parents divorced. It messed everything up."

"My dad died and I didn't want to bother my mom. I had no one to talk to."

"My parents were alcoholics."

"My mom beat up my sisters and me."

"I couldn't stand all the pressure to be perfect in everything I did."

"I wasn't fitting in at school. I had no friends and felt really lonely."

"My girlfriend dumped me."

"I honestly don't know why I do it. I just feel empty inside."

Christian Hill, a Colorado Springs-based counselor who meets with many teens who have self-injured, says, "Rarely is the driving force behind cutting as clean as we would like it to be. Usually it's a combination of several things." Emotions overwhelm, depression or anxiety settle in, pain and disillusionment become too much to bear.

For these young people, just as with Jackie, at the time of such intense feelings, hurting themselves seemed to be the only way to cope. When asked what it did for them, they added:

"It calmed me down."

"It gets my mind off of emotional stuff."

"I felt like I'm the one in control instead of everyone else."

"It helped me feel like I'm here—like I am living and maybe I matter."

"When I did it, I could escape my fears and anxieties."

"My scars remind me that my past is real."

"It's the only pain I could control."

"I felt like I was bad, like I needed to punish myself."

"I did it to survive. Otherwise, I might have ended my life."

> Everyone needs people in life who will honor and encourage the person they are becoming, who care about what they think or feel. Someone who has turned to self-harming behavior may not have experienced enough of these kinds of relationships. Maybe you're one who can begin to provide that kind of support for a friend or family member who self-injures.

GETTING GOD IN THE PICTURE

Emotions are amazingly intense. Some of yours might tie your painful past to the present situations in your life. You might not know how to begin to talk about the feelings, thoughts, and memories. You're not alone. A huge number of those who hurt themselves to cope with their emotions have communication difficulties in their homes.

Susan Bowman, author of *See My Pain*, a book on strategies for those who self-injure, says that we tend to model ourselves after the people in our lives who haven't known how to talk about personal problems or feelings.

Susan Cook, a counselor who has met with teens and young adults who self-injure, adds that pain as a life circumstance "is just not something we're talking about enough with kids"—

especially in the church. She says, "You're going to get the impression there's something wrong with you because you feel intense pain."

The need to talk is there, but you may feel like no one wants to listen. Confusion slithers its way in when people try to change what you feel or what you remember and make your feelings seem like nothing. They don't understand, or they aren't sure how to handle your emotions. "Get over it," they might say. "Suck it up and be a man." "Well, we just don't talk about those things."

The silencing brings yet another pain that's difficult to overcome—shame. Your thoughts and emotions seem unacceptable to others, so how could they understand why you hurt yourself? Shame is at least partly what turns your self-harm into a secret that you hide under long pants and sleeves.

Your thoughts, feelings, and memories *are* important and deserve to be heard. You don't have to keep quiet or hide.

In Genesis 3, you can read about the first man and woman on earth, Adam and Eve. They're known for feeling ashamed and hiding. Lured by Satan, they disobeyed God. When shame enveloped them, they covered themselves and hid. Later, when they heard God calling them in the garden, they were terrified. But they didn't need to be afraid. What he wanted most was to bring them out of their shame and back into his arms.

I don't know where you've got God in the picture, but I encourage you to let him into your life now more than you ever have. He knows all the details. He knows what has happened and what you feel. You can tell him what makes you angry, sad, lonely, scared, anxious, or ashamed. You can talk about the memories and situations in your life that caused your greatest pain. He won't tell you to be quiet. He won't leave you in your shame. He can take it away.

And those things you don't understand or remember right now—if they're important, God will take you through them at the right time. What he has in mind for you is your total healing, from the inside out. He will help you write the next chapters of your unique story and take it in an amazing direction—one that isn't filled with a pain that's impossible to handle on your own. He'll carry it for you, if you let him.

Jesus, you are there waiting for me to come with the pain, the terrifying memories, the expectations I have of myself and that others have of me—all those things I think and feel and have held inside. I can come to you because you've already come to me. You are waiting to listen in a way others haven't yet been able to. I'm glad you won't turn away or make me feel stupid. You won't look at me with disgust. In your eyes, I am lovable. Today, help me learn to trust you and let you into my life more, especially at those moments when I want to hurt myself. Help me begin to understand how to live differently, how to live free. AMEN.

He heals the brokenhearted and binds up their wounds.
PSALM 147:3

GOING DEEPER

- Maybe you behave in ways—through self-injury or otherwise—that you don't understand and leave you feeling ashamed. In what ways has this prevented you from talking to God about what you think and feel?

- Since God is always willing to welcome you into a relationship with him and since he won't tell you to be quiet—think again about the message of Psalm 147:3—what could you tell him right now about what's happening to you?

- What feels impossible for you to handle on your own? What specific action can you take to invite God to carry it for you?

DEEPER STILL

Using your favorite art materials, create a picture of your life as you see it now. Then consider how God can become a part of that depiction and draw him into your picture. Make your artwork a form of prayer inviting God into what's happening in your life.

two

I cut, and I just put a Band-Aid on them and forget.
They are covered and in time they heal. No one knows.
I'm hurt. No one knows.

—Jackie's Journal

"HEY, ANYONE WANT THE LAST TACO?" Jackie held up a cardboard take-out box.

The large room, part gym and part social hall, of Ceres Christian Church echoed with the sounds of the last slurps of sodas and crumpling wrappers of a fast food meal. At a round table in the center of the room, Jackie and four other high school students finished off their dinner of tacos and Mexican pizza.

Melody shuffled through her notes and whisked blond strands of hair away from her face. "OK, I think we've covered everything. Our retreat is planned, and we've got this month's outreaches set—the graffiti cleanup and the Bible class for the shelter kids." She looked up at her student leaders. Her vivid green eyes, with their perfectly applied makeup, focused on Jackie. "Would you like to close in prayer?"

Jackie was glad to be asked. "Sure." She bowed her head; the others followed. "God, help things go well tonight during youth meeting. Help everyone be open to you. And help us with all our activities in the community. Amen."

She stacked her discipleship study guide on top of her Bible. At fifteen and close to the end of her freshman year of high school, Jackie felt happy to be part of the leadership team.

Thursdays were good. She looked forward to the worship times, to laughing with her friends in leadership, to praying for others at the youth meeting. But tonight other thoughts were dogging her.

What about yesterday? What would everyone think if they knew that I—

Doors crashed open and Jackie jerked her attention to the rest of the youth group, which was now pouring into the room. Within moments a basketball game had broken out on the blue outdoor carpet laid down in the gym, and a shot whooshed through the hoop. Friends greeted each other and mixed in groups around the room. Jackie joined the others clearing trash left over from their dinner and helped Anna and Danielle push their meeting table out of the middle of the hoops court.

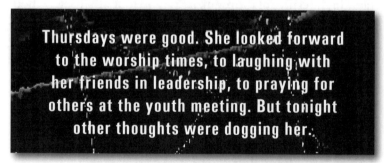

Thursdays were good. She looked forward to the worship times, to laughing with her friends in leadership, to praying for others at the youth meeting. But tonight other thoughts were dogging her.

"It's so cool doing the Bible studies at the shelter," said Anna, another student leader. "The kids always seem so excited we're there. I can't wait."

"Yeah," Danielle agreed. "The graffiti cleanup's hard work, but it's cool too. Jackie, you going to go?"

"Yeah. Probably."

"Hey guys, it's ten till. Youth group's about ready to start," Melody called across the room. "Let's go."

The basketball bounced a few more times, then rolled to the corner. The students joined up in groups to walk through the foyer between the social hall and the sanctuary. Jackie stepped into the crowd heading into the church, and she and the other leaders mixed into the first three rows of excited junior high and high schoolers. Talk continued through the hall as the worship band tuned up. The drummer hammered out a set of beats while the bass player ran his fingers down the neck of his Fender Jazz.

A prayer and a few announcements, and the group of more than fifty youth finally got quiet. Soon the room vibrated with a chorus of "Hold me close, let your love surround me. Bring me near, draw me to your side" . . . Around her, kids linked hands. Some knelt in front of their pews while they worshiped God. Jackie closed her eyes and sang, as if in prayer.

Her voice began to break.

God, I want that kind of power. I want to know your love, but I'm not worthy of it.

The longing was too much. Tears began to stream down Jackie's face. She opened her eyes. Several had come to the front and knelt at the steps leading to the stage. A week ago she had been one of those who had come up front for prayer. Melody had slipped up beside her, placed her hand on her shoulder, and prayed for her. Other adult leaders who knew her gathered around her and prayed. Jackie cried that night too—a lot.

You were there, God. I felt your peace. It's been a whole week now since I cut myself. God, help me.

two

Jackie sighed and opened her eyes. For now she could at least pray for someone else. She moved toward the front and sat next to Amy, one of the eighth-grade girls, who talked about her struggle with peer pressure and making good choices. Jackie knew what that felt like. She prayed out loud: "Bring good friends into Amy's life, and give her strength. Help her trust you and know what to do."

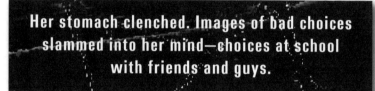

Her stomach clenched. Images of bad choices slammed into her mind—choices at school with friends and guys.

Help me know too, God.

How far short she fell from that knowledge. Her stomach clenched. Images of bad choices slammed into her mind— choices at school with friends and guys.

Can I ever change? I don't think anyone believes I can. God, do you think that too?

Her thoughts flashed to the day before; she cringed. Five of her friends wanted to skip a couple classes. The school didn't have gates or fences, so it was easy to sneak off. Jackie had no problem joining her friends. She hated school.

They had left campus, driven around awhile, and then pulled up to a park. Before they got out of the car, they saw the tagged picnic tables and the graffiti sprayed across the bathroom buildings. Guys in their early twenties leaned against metal tables under a green shade canopy. Jackie noticed their tattoos and colors and realized she and her friends were in gang territory. Still, the girls walked their way.

SCARS THAT WOUND : SCARS THAT HEAL

The next hour turned into a blur of drinking and flirting. One guy began to cuss about one girl's shirt and shoes being in colors another gang would wear. The situation got out of control fast, so Jackie and her friends left. She asked them to drop her off at home. She didn't want to go back to school. Teachers probably were beginning to guess she was starting to get high a lot of the time, but they didn't need to see her drunk.

Now, tonight, Jackie shuddered at that memory.

God, should I even be here praying for this girl? I'm one person here and a different person away from the youth group.

Prayer and worship time ended. Everybody settled into their seats, ready to hear the lesson. Tonight's talk was about peer pressure and staying away from drinking and drugs. *It figures,* Jackie thought. Melody's voice wove in and out of Jackie's thoughts.

"It's a choice. You can say no," Melody was saying.

Sounds so easy. Why can't I do it?

After youth group, Jackie helped clean up, then joined the others in the parking lot. For now, she would put aside the conflicting emotions and laugh and enjoy the conversation. One by one, the others left as parents arrived to take them home. Though Jackie lived only a few blocks away, she always waited for a ride from Melody.

From across the lot, Jackie saw Melody leaving the church, so she headed for her car. She slid into the passenger seat, shut the door, and pulled her seat belt around her.

"Youth group went pretty well tonight," Melody said as she started the engine.

"Yeah, it was good." Jackie didn't feel much like talking.

"How's school going?"

"OK." Jackie shifted in her seat and stared out the window. The car pulled out of the parking lot, and she watched the familiar scenes pass across her view: a funeral home, the row of buses at the elementary school, the neighborhood houses.

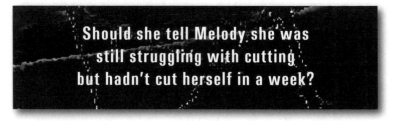

Should she tell Melody she was still struggling with cutting but hadn't cut herself in a week?

Melody slowed the car and Jackie felt her youth pastor watching her. Waiting for a deeper response.

Jackie shifted and let her head fall back against the seat. "OK, I've been drinking sometimes." She shut her eyes and drew in a breath. Should she tell Melody she was still struggling with cutting but hadn't cut herself in a week—that the prayers for her had helped? Her stomach twisted in a knot.

"Drinking? Recently?" Melody asked.

"Yesterday. I ditched school and went to some park in Modesto." The guilt she felt over her double life felt claustrophobic. She could hardly choke out a response, but gradually she told Melody what happened.

Melody pulled the car to the curb in front of Jackie's house.

"What do you feel about it now?"

"I shouldn't have done it." She really believed that and she wished she could live straight. Melody didn't even know about the drugs, but she probably had already guessed Jackie was

SCARS THAT WOUND : SCARS THAT HEAL

starting to do stuff that she shouldn't with guys. All of it got her through, helping her block out the unrelenting anxiety.

"Have you prayed and let God help you? I mean *really* let him?" Melody asked.

She had let Melody down. Again. She stared at her clenched hands in her lap as warm tears slid down her cheeks. "I'm such a loser. I'm so messed up. I don't deserve—"

Melody touched Jackie's shoulder. "We all struggle and God doesn't look at any of us that way." They sat in silence for a couple of minutes before Melody asked, "What can I do to help?"

Jackie's shoulder's lifted and fell in a shrug. She wished there was something Melody could do, that *anyone* could do to make things better.

Melody hugged Jackie. "You know I love you and I'm praying for you."

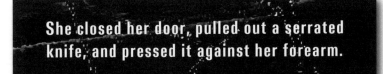

She closed her door, pulled out a serrated knife, and pressed it against her forearm.

Jackie nodded.

"You're going to be OK."

Jackie let out a deep breath and opened the door. "Bye, Melody."

"See you on Sunday. Call me anytime you need to."

The tiny yellow porch light barely lit the pathway to the door. Its glow felt as dull and far away as the peace she had experienced at last week's youth night. If only she could recapture that feeling and somehow carry it with her. Now all she felt was the heaviness of guilt over her choices.

She walked through the house toward her bedroom, barely mumbling a greeting to her parents.

She closed her door, pulled out a serrated knife, and pressed it against her forearm.

> In certain ways we are weak, but the Spirit is here to help us. For example, when we don't know what to pray for, the Spirit prays for us in ways that cannot be put into words.
>
> ROMANS 8:26 (CEV)

HELP ME FEEL NORMAL

The prayer time Jackie had experienced the week before was genuine. God's presence was real. But the emotions inside still crashed like waves against all that felt wrong in her life. By this point Jackie was using drugs, alcohol, and self-injury to try to make sense of her tangled inner world. And just after she turned fifteen, she started sleeping around with guys.

At church she presented a different Jackie—one she liked a little better. For a short time each week, she felt happy, normal, worthwhile. She later said, "I was always really excited that I got to participate in youth leadership—a real, deep-down excitement. I felt a sense that this is what God had for me. At the same time, I felt extremely guilty about how I lived outside of church."

Jackie and the other leadership kids put together devotions that they presented in small groups. "Jackie was great at that,"

Melody recalled. "Kids begged to be in her group. She was fun, and they saw her as a great prayer warrior. What she was doing at church was sincere, though she was struggling."

Melody's picture of Jackie's life away from church was limited. She knew how hard it was at home for her young friend, so she focused on keeping her involved and holding on to hope. When it became clearer that her struggles were deepening, Melody had to weigh the impact of Jackie's actions on the rest of the youth. Looking back, Melody recalled, "I knew we might have to take her out of leadership." She realized it would be a tough call. "Jackie was looking for unconditional love and crying out for help. We needed to be full of love and compassion—but also real firm."

Some wonder if the person who self-injures is manipulating people to get attention. His self-harming behavior can be a cry for help. What he needs most is your respect and compassion.

Jackie's close friends and church family didn't know about the early secrets that had taken root and carved lies into her mind. As a child, she had been molested multiple times, by five different people. She was betrayed, violated, and left with a twisted sense of who she was and what was normal. By fifteen, the memories were overshadowed by a mixed-up blur of anxiety and anger.

Then it happened again. A boy Jackie knew from the youth group attacked her while she was home alone. She felt helpless and terrified. She finally got him to leave and phoned for help.

"I was in shock," Jackie remembered. "My mom came home from work early and Melody came over. They were both really angry at the guy, and they wanted to make sure I was OK. We went to the station, and I had to tell a policeman what happened. He only made it an assault since he [the boy] didn't rape me." For once she spoke up, but she felt ignored and belittled. She wished she hadn't reported it.

Time passed, and the people who had supported her seemed to forget. Jackie couldn't. Besides, something else stuck with her. When she told her dad what happened, he said she shouldn't have worn that spaghetti strap dress to church. She believed him—she had brought it on, she told herself.

All the betrayals and violations screamed a clear message: "You deserve to be treated this way. Bad things happen to bad people. You're not worth anything."

She would either try to make sense of that message or silence it.

Drugs.

Do I deserve what's happened to me? Please, someone, tell me it's not true.

Alcohol.

I don't want to hear anymore. I don't want to feel.

Sex.

I do matter. Don't I?

Self-injury.

So much inside. Will you listen? Will you care?

Hiding.

I'm hurt. No one knows.

Confusion. Pain. Lies.

On some level you might relate to Jackie. You might not. Whatever your story, the emotions and pain you guard are personal and real. But hiding has a downside. It's a lot of work to keep secrets all the time. Many who self-injure grow weary of the constant concealment.

Shauna, whose self-abuse included cutting and anorexia, told her counselor life was great. But as she wrote in her journal, "It was how I wished things were. Am I really that good at faking it? She told me how proud she was of me. Shouldn't she be able to see past my lies?"

Others played the role they wanted people to believe. Dan was determined to pull off the impression he had everything together. Neither Callie nor Ryan wanted anyone to think they were crazy. Alisa refused to appear weak or needy. Kyle made jokes to keep everyone laughing so others would think he was happy. Jordan grieved alone over the loss of a close friend; no one would find out he was carving on himself to cope with it.

Jena often cut herself. "At home I'd be crying all day, keeping everything to myself, having all these feelings and thoughts rise up in my mind," she said. "At church or out with anyone else, I was happy and giddy. It gets really old trying to act OK for people. Eventually your smile just doesn't have any meaning."

If you wrote the same words in your journal that Jackie wrote—"No one knows. I'm hurt. No one knows"—would you be talking about the fresh cut or burn, or the pain inside?

Become the kind of person that someone who self-injures can feel safe with and trust. Be a good listener, be patient, and be honest. You can say, "I may not ever fully understand, but I'm here to listen."

OUT IN THE LIGHT

Whatever the secrets—created by you or laid on you through crazy and painful circumstances—Psalm 139 has a freeing reminder. Nothing is done in secret. Someone knows and cares—God.

He knew all about you even before you were fashioned so intricately in the womb. He knows every day of your life at a depth and with a love that honors all of who he created you to be. He is acutely aware of every moment of pain, anger, or weakness you may feel. And he doesn't condemn you. When you've shed a tear or a drop of blood and thought you were alone, you were not. He was there even in those places that felt so dark and hopeless.

Another thing about God—it's his design to work through the people who love him to remind you of his presence and love. If you ask him, he'll bring someone into your life to help you tell your story and discover healing in the telling.

Alisa told her story to someone she learned to trust. "Talking brings everything out of the darkness into the light," she said. "It's scary, but it's part of the healing." Karley said that beginning to share her secrets was what finally set her free. "I

SCARS THAT WOUND : SCARS THAT HEAL

had to get my self-injury out in the open to be able to have God's light shine on it and find some help." Said Kyle, "Bringing it out in the open is what brought me back to church and ultimately to a new and better relationship with God."

Being real with others and God can begin to change your life dramatically. Ephesians 5:8 says, "For you were formerly darkness, but now you are Light in the Lord; walk as children of Light." Wow. Outside of a relationship with God, living in our own secrets that are far from God's design for us, we're choosing to live in darkness. Going to him, who is Light, we gain an amazing identity.

Take that in. To be a child of Light has been his intention for you all along.

God, you really know me. You're aware of everything that's happened to me and the crazy lies I've come to believe about myself and about this world I live in. You are here with me now. You know everything I'm thinking, saying, and doing, but in a way that really values who I am and who you created me to be. Help me walk out of the shadows of my secrets and find someone trustworthy to talk to. Give me courage to tell the whole truth of my story. When I do, help me trust you with any feelings that may make me want to hurt myself. Free me from darkness and make me your child of light. AMEN.

"For I know the plans I have for you," declares the Lord, "plans to prosper you and not to harm you, plans to give you hope and a future. Then you will call upon me and come and pray to me, and I will listen to you. You will seek me and find me when you seek me with all your heart."

JEREMIAH 29:11-13 (NIV)

GOING DEEPER

- Secrets only heap more pain onto an already difficult situation. What secrets do you long to be able to face, to let others know about?

- God designed you to be a child of light. How would you describe any darkness you may have been living in? Compare it with the light God wants you to experience.

- In truth, no secrets exist with God. If you let him, he will be with you as you begin to bring your self-injury into the open. What positive step can you take today?

DEEPER STILL

Write an honest prayer to God about your self-injury and what others may not know. To begin to bring your self-injury into the light, ask God to show you someone you can talk with about what you're feeling. Consider sharing your written prayer with that person.

three

I'm trying to stay really calm. I hate feeling this angry,
where I feel like I'm going to go out of control.

—Jackie's Journal

"Braaaaaaaaawrrrrp."

"Eeeraahrrrrrrrrrrrp."

Each of the two leadership guys downed more Dr Pepper and made his best efforts to beat the other's long, loud burps. Jackie laughed as she pulled a chair out from the table and sat down to watch the contest play out.

"Come on, it's your turn," the guys said, trying to get the girls into the competition.

Jackie's sophomore year of high school was drawing to a close, and this was the first night of the church's annual youth leadership retreat. The brown carpet and tan, orange, and gold plaid furniture gave the rented Sierra foothills cabin an '80s feel. Maybe '70s. Something old, anyway.

Jackie thought about all the planning they had put into this retreat. They'd not only scheduled lots of prayer time but also intended to squeeze in a visit to nearby historic Columbia, a town founded during the California Gold Rush. Jackie hoped they wouldn't do the picture thing—posing as a group for one of those old-fashioned photos. Whatever. At least everyone would have fun hanging out. And they had plenty to eat. She knew because she had helped with the menus.

The burps continued and one of the girls launched into an imitation of some crazy Jim Carrey character. Jackie watched and laughed. It was cool that everyone was wearing the T-shirts she had helped create. Across each cotton shirt was the saying "Those who die with the most toys win." "The most toys" was X-ed out using a red cross, and the word Jesus was written just below.

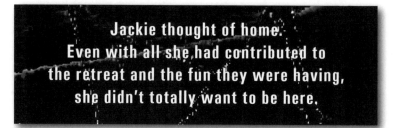

Jackie thought of home. Even with all she had contributed to the retreat and the fun they were having, she didn't totally want to be here.

Melody's husband, Tom, picked up his guitar and began tuning it. He wore his usual jeans and the retreat T-shirt. His green eyes and black moustache stood out against his dark, Portuguese complexion. Grabbing a chair and setting it toward the couches, he raised his voice above the laughter ripping through the cabin. "Hey guys, let's hang out over here." The guys joked and punched each other as they straggled toward Tom, then plopped down in various spots on the floor in front of him.

Jackie stayed in her chair at the table. One of the newer girls sat down next to her. As Tom began playing a few worship songs, Jackie thought of home. Even with all she had contributed to the retreat and the fun they were having, she didn't totally want to be here. She had almost backed out. The leadership group had recently doubled to six teen leaders, including Jackie, and she didn't know some of the others. Last year's retreat felt more comfortable with Melody, Jackie, and a couple other girls. As stressful as home felt, she wished she were there right now.

She watched Tom nod to Melody as he finished his last song. Melody moved near Tom and said, "Before we pray for each of you individually, do you have any prayer requests?" A few shared personal struggles and concerns. Jackie remained quiet.

"OK, let's pray." Melody and Tom stepped toward one of the guys. Melody touched the top of his head while Tom placed his hand on Josh's shoulder. Jackie tensed. Would she be next? She listened to Tom and Melody's words.

"Empower Josh to be the leader you've called him to be. Use the gifts and talents you've given him to make a difference in the lives of the others in his life . . ."

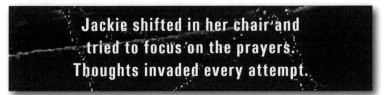

Jackie shifted in her chair and
tried to focus on the prayers.
Thoughts invaded every attempt.

Jackie tightened her arms around herself. *Are they going to pray for me like that? I don't deserve it.*

Tom and Melody moved to the next person on the floor. Jackie shifted in her chair and tried to focus on the prayers. Thoughts invaded every attempt.

I'm getting high almost every day. Do they know? I want to leave.

"Help Anna as she adjusts to her parents' divorce. As she stays at each of their houses, let her know that you are with her . . ."

three

Prayer doesn't work for me. I've tried, and I'm still cutting every week. I'm never going to change. They shouldn't pray for me. She hoped Melody and Tom would forget she was there.

She watched them move toward the next person in the circle.

Melody. Her youth pastor cared— but things had changed between them.

Why did I come? Do I even want this church stuff anymore? I believe in Jesus, but I can't live like I'm supposed to.

The prayers continued. "Help Danielle love you more and more each day . . ."

Their words faded into the background of Jackie's thoughts. *I don't know how I'm even alive. I'm hanging out with some pretty crazy people. Getting high, sleeping around . . . I probably have some disease that will kill me. If not, I'll probably die overdosing.*

" . . . help her be strong and know your joy."

I wish I could stop all the bad stuff I'm doing, but I don't know how. Besides, how would I get through the day? No, I can't stop. It won't work. It feels too . . .

Melody and Tom were already around the circle and praying for the new girl, Kristi, sitting next to Jackie.

Melody. Her youth pastor cared—but things had changed between them.

I can't tell her stuff like I used to, and Mom won't let me hang out with my school friends much anymore. OK, she's right. We get messed up in a lot of bad stuff. But I need to talk to someone.

Melody and Tom stood in front of Jackie. Each placed a hand on one of her shoulders.

Melody started to pray. Jackie felt her skin grow warm. Her stomach clenched.

"God, help Jackie become strong against peer pressure. Strengthen her each day in all she struggles with. She has so many gifts to share. Give her the desire to use them and to grow in leadership . . ."

Jackie felt her legs shaking. *I don't want this. I can't take the guilt I'm feeling. Stop praying for me. Please, stop praying.*

The words stopped. Her shaking didn't. Her eyes were filling with tears. Had Tom and Melody noticed?

As soon as the prayer ended and everyone got up again, Jackie escaped to the bathroom at the top of the stairs. She closed the door firmly behind her and spun toward the sink. Tears now flowed from the large brown eyes staring back at her from the mirror.

What am I doing? Those people downstairs care about me. God does too. One moment I want all that and the next, I want to get as far away as possible.

Her heart beat fast. In the mirror, she watched the quick rise and fall of her breathing. Her eyes grew round as her anxiety rose like a rushing river overflowing its banks.

Make the feelings stop.

She spotted a pink razor on the edge of the sink. She picked it up.

Why do I want to do this so bad?

She didn't know; she only knew she had no idea how to fight it. She made slashes across her left arm, beginning at her wrist and moving up her forearm. She stood in front of the sink, crying and cutting for twenty minutes. Each second and each

three

cut brought more relief. Relaxation settled in—then, finally, numbness.

A knock at the door made her jump. She couldn't face anyone now. She wanted to escape out the window—escape forever.

"Jackie, are you OK?"

"Come on, open the door."

The voices belonged to Danielle and Anna.

She stared at the marks on her arm. *What will they do if they see this?*

"Jackie?"

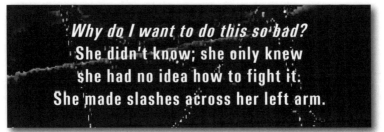

Why do I want to do this so bad? She didn't know; she only knew she had no idea how to fight it. She made slashes across her left arm.

Fear squeezed every inch of her, but she knew that if she stalled, they'd just keep asking questions. She opened the door and watched their expressions as their eyes moved from her face to her arms. Their concern began to turn into irritation.

"Jackie, what are you doing?"

"Are you trying to kill yourself?"

The two girls looked at each other. "Should we tell Tom and Melody?" Danielle asked.

"Please don't," Jackie begged. "I'll be OK."

Danielle and Anna left and Jackie closed the bathroom door again. She cleaned her arms and covered the fresh cuts with the sleeves of her sweatshirt before she headed downstairs.

The next few hours were agonizing. Were the girls going to tell or not? Had they already? Jackie waited.

Finally, Melody approached Jackie. "Let's go out on the porch," Melody said. Once there, she faced Jackie and put her hands on her arms. "I love you and I'm afraid for you. At some point you're going to cut too deep."

"I'm not trying to kill myself. I'll be OK," Jackie answered.

"All right, I won't take you home. We'll stay for the rest of the retreat."

That's it? Jackie didn't think so.

After the retreat, Tom and Melody drove Jackie home. On the way they told her they would go inside with her. Her parents needed to know what had happened.

Jackie knew this wouldn't go well. She was disappointing everyone again. Tears were already burning her eyes.

The three stepped through the front doorway, with Jackie in the lead. Mom looked up from her place on the couch as they entered the living room. Dad and Nikki walked in from the back of the house. Nikki, thirteen and full of attitude, raised her eyebrows when she saw Jackie with Tom and Melody. She tossed her curly, black hair, leaned against the wall, and glared.

Dad cast a big grin at everyone; he seemed clueless about where this was heading. "How was the retreat?"

Mom looked from Melody to Jackie, and Jackie watched the familiar signs of anger appear in her mother's narrowed eyes and tightened lips.

"What's going on?" Mom asked Melody. She turned to Jackie. "What did you do this time?"

While Melody began to explain, Tom walked over and leaned on the arm of the couch where Jackie's mom was sitting. Everyone else stood while Melody related what happened at the retreat. Finally, she finished. ". . . Then Jackie got upset at the retreat and cut her arm."

Questions and comments flew from all parts of the room.

"Why would you do something like that?"

"Were you trying to kill yourself?"

"She just wants attention."

"She could have died."

"Are you OK? What should we do?"

"I thought you stopped this behavior."

"We need to do something."

"Maybe she needs to go the hospital."

Then . . . silence.

Nikki rolled her eyes and walked out of the room.

Melody spoke. "The hospital might be the best solution."

Mom and Dad nodded.

Tom went to the phone to make some calls. Jackie waited in the uncomfortable silence. Then she began to walk toward the back of the house.

Jackie's mom sat up. "Where are you going?"

"Just to the bathroom." *Do they actually think I'll do something now?*

Melody began to follow. "I'll go."

Jackie let out a sigh. "I won't do anything." Melody went with her anyway.

As Melody and Jackie returned to the living room, Tom hung up the phone. "Memorial Hospital says Jackie should come

 SCARS THAT WOUND : SCARS THAT HEAL

in for an evaluation. Fred, Betty, you need to take her. Melody and I can drive if you'd like."

At the hospital, Jackie sat on the edge of an ER bed while a counselor sat in a nearby chair. He crossed his legs and scribbled notes about their conversation. Jackie guessed the man, dressed in a buttoned-up shirt and slacks, was in his forties. She detected a slight accent as he asked her questions about her family and what had happened at the cabin. He was kind. She willingly talked about the stresses of home.

"Sounds like you've got a lot going on," the counselor said. "You've hurt yourself, and I'm not sure how far you might have taken that. I'm not sure you are either." He paused and watched her for a moment. "I'm recommending that you go to the behavioral center." He flipped through his notepad. "You'll need to ride in an ambulance, but you can see your parents when you get there."

She detected a slight accent as he asked her questions about her family and what had happened at the cabin. He was kind. She willingly talked about the stresses of home.

Jackie mustered a response. "OK." Thoughts poured through her mind. *How are Mom and Dad feeling? What will a mental hospital be like? How long will I be there? Can I see my family?* She didn't want to think anymore. She felt nauseous, tired.

The hospital attendants escorted Jackie to the ambulance that would take her to the behavioral center. Her parents and

Tom and Melody followed. Outside they met the paramedics, who explained that Jackie wouldn't need physical monitoring even though they considered her "5150"—the code for suicidal, in danger of harming oneself. An escort was needed, she was told, but Jackie could sit for the ride. Jackie felt too weary to try to convince yet another person that she wasn't about to kill herself.

"Your parents will go with us and we'll follow," Melody told Jackie.

She nodded and climbed in through the rear doors of the ambulance. Jackie took a seat behind the driver and faced the back window, which gave a view of the fast-approaching nightfall. As the ambulance pulled out, she scanned the street for Tom and Melody's SUV. Once she spotted their red Blazer, she watched nothing else for the entire trip to the mental hospital.

> Create in me a clean heart, O God,
> and renew a steadfast spirit within me.
>
> PSALM 51:10

WHY COULDN'T SHE JUST STOP?

For Jackie's family and friends, her cutting stirred up a whirlwind of emotions and questions. Each person wanted her to be OK. Some wanted a quick fix. Jackie waited in the eye of the storm, hoping she'd make it through. She wanted answers even more than they did.

It was one of the toughest weekends of Jackie's young life. "Everyone was in shock because they had no idea I was still hurting myself," she remembered later.

Melody, who had never heard of self-injury until she met Jackie, thought the worst. For her, cutting your arms and wrists only added up to one thing—a suicide attempt. "It really hit me how distraught Jackie was and that she was crying out for help," Melody recalled. "It scared me for her."

Jackie's mom looked back on that time and remembered feeling afraid for Jackie and unsure about what should happen next. "I didn't know why she would do something like that, why she couldn't just stop. I had no comprehension at all of what she was going through. Her answer of 'I don't know' was so frustrating."

Jackie's parents hesitated at first to send her to the treatment center, but then thought it could be what she needed. "We didn't understand her cutting," Betty said. "In our opinion she should just stop, but obviously she needed help. We were praying she would find help, hoping that the treatment center was something that would be good for her. It's sad to see your daughter in an ambulance heading to a mental health ward. Our view of the mental hospital at that time was that it was for really crazy people, and we didn't consider Jackie crazy."

Jackie's mom struggled with some anger at the time. But looking back, she's fought plenty of tears. She also had a mother's deep instincts of care, even if she struggled with how to show it. "I felt scared for her because I couldn't imagine what she was going through—being in an ambulance, going to a place she doesn't know—all the things a mother feels for a daughter."

Jackie had been quiet while her parents and Tom and Melody talked through the hospital option. But a lot was going through her mind. "I didn't think I needed the mental hospital, but at the same time, I didn't know what I needed," she recalled. "It was like 'OK, whatever you guys think is best.'" Since she was going whether she wanted to or not, she only hoped someone there could tell her why she was depressed and hurting herself.

Today, most of Jackie's seventy-two-hour stay in the hospital is blocked from her memory. She remembers that the staff put her on antidepressants and recommended a program to help her and her parents learn to communicate better. Maybe it would work, she thought at the time, but after her release, Jackie didn't understand her self-injury any better. In her mind, her stay only cemented another mistaken concept of who she was. "I just thought I was crazy, and that I was going to be crazy for the rest of my life."

A person who harms herself may be trying to cope so she doesn't turn to suicide instead. Continue to support and listen carefully and be aware of warning signs. Never hesitate to get professional or pastoral help if you're concerned suicide might be a possibility.

DUMPING THE CONFUSION

Misconceptions about self-injury abound. Many don't understand it and often form perceptions that are way off target. Then, if you're already carrying your own load of feelings about your self-injury and the possibilities for healing,

SCARS THAT WOUND : SCARS THAT HEAL

frustration can mount. You get an even bigger mess when you add in confusing beliefs about God.

Jackie believed she was a loser. Other messages she told herself included "I can never change," "I deserve all the bad stuff that's happened to me," "I don't matter," "prayer doesn't work for me," and "I must be crazy." She believed God didn't like her and had plenty of reasons not to. She continued to struggle with that one quite often.

All of the above are common feelings for the self-injurer.

Jena said, "I was mad at God for making me, for letting the situations in my life happen, even for the family I was in. I tried to convince myself that he hated me, he hated my body, and that he wanted nothing to do with me. I knew inside of me that he loved me no matter what had happened. It was my own thoughts that confused me."

Ericka's mom used the Bible to show her how bad she was. "That's what made me terrified of God," Ericka said. She so thoroughly believed her "badness" that she felt whatever she touched, physically or emotionally, would be destroyed. But fortunately, she was able to challenge many of those beliefs. Recently she said, "I haven't cut for four months. My mom and I are amazing. God is working."

Alisa thought God would never accept her because of her "dirty secret" of self-injury and that, even if he did, he couldn't help her. She said, "I felt the pain too deeply, and God wasn't big enough to deal with self-injury or heal me from it." Later, when she began to get well, she became more and more confident that "I am a child of God. He is a big God. He can deal with any situation and heal me from the pain."

Dan struggled with reopening his wounds and not allowing his scabs to heal. While he was growing up he believed that God was distant and that he—and the people in Dan's life—required perfection from him. That changed. Dan came to find out that "God doesn't expect perfection from me. God loves me, scabs, scars, and all. . . . His image of me matters way more than my own, faulty self-image. I've had to work to get my self-concept from him, to understand that I am 'fearfully and wonderfully made'" (Psalm 139:14).

> Someone who self-harms may say "I'm a cutter" or "I'm a self-injurer." Help him discover who he is apart from his harming behavior. For one, he can be a child of God.

MESSAGES YOU CAN TRUST

Jena, Ericka, Alisa, and Dan all discovered some excellent truths about themselves and about God. They realized their view of him wasn't entirely accurate, and that God's view of them and what they were able to handle was vastly different from what they had thought. They all had to recognize they couldn't wait until someone else in their lives understood what was going on with them. Instead, they took the step of challenging their misconceptions about themselves, their self-injury, and God. They found a fantastic source to challenge those misconceptions—the Bible.

Sometimes others tell you what the Bible says, and they mean well. But the end result can be that, like Ericka's mom, they get it wrong. She missed what God really wanted her daughter to know: Every one of us falls short in light of his goodness and perfection, but God delights in lavishing us with his love and forgiveness when we ask him to be a part of our life (Titus 3:3-7; Ephesians 1:7, 8; 1 Timothy 1:15, 16).

So check out God's words for yourself. Pray that he helps you understand them. If something doesn't make sense and seems to give you a conflicting view, don't settle for another misconception. Wait and keep praying for God to show you the truth. Here are a few of his messages for you and where you can find them in the Bible:

You were beautifully and purposefully created,
not mistakenly or horribly so (Psalm 139:14).

If you are in Christ, he sees a new beginning
in you (2 Corinthians 5:17).

You were designed for honor and for good
(Ephesians 2:10; 2 Timothy 2:21).

God invites you to be adopted into his family and
enjoy an amazing inheritance (Ephesians 1:3-12).

Turn to these truths from the Bible when you're struggling with understanding what God is all about—especially in how he views you and the healing he desires for you. You can trust his words.

God, thank you that you see clearly who I am, and that I can trust your view of me. Help me become more and more open to learning the truth about you, about myself, and about the possibilities for my healing. Help me recognize quickly when I'm hearing or thinking something that is not true. You really are a big God with great thoughts in mind for me, and nothing I've faced or will face is too much for you to handle. AMEN.

> Therefore if anyone is in Christ, he is a new creature; the old things passed away; behold, new things have come.
>
> 2 CORINTHIANS 5:17

GOING DEEPER

- Sometimes we create labels for ourselves, like "I'm a cutter." Try saying instead, "I'm a child of God." How might that make a difference in the moment you're living right now?

- Holding on to misconceptions about God, or self, only adds more pain to a person's life. What view of God, or yourself, needs confronting head-on?

- Getting God involved in your journey out of self-injury will make an amazing difference. What are a few specific ways you can include him in your growth and healing?

DEEPER STILL

Choose some of the Bible verses from this chapter or find others that are meaningful to you. Write them on index cards and add statements that are important to you, like "God sees me as his creation, a beautiful work of art; he loves me." Keep the cards where you'll see them every day.

four

The anxiety is still pretty intense.
I want to hurt myself so bad. Having to fight off
these thoughts and feelings is driving me crazy.

—Jackie's Journal

THE BREEZE FROM THE OPEN CAR WINDOW played with the loose strands of Jackie's long dark hair. As she tucked them back under her hair clip, she sighed. A month and a half had passed since she came home from the hospital. Maybe she was finally free of the vigilant watching and staring.

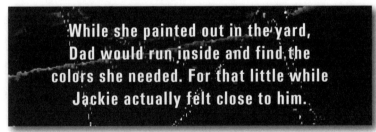

While she painted out in the yard, Dad would run inside and find the colors she needed. For that little while Jackie actually felt close to him.

Today Jackie and her youth group were headed to the beach. Her mom, as one of the youth sponsors, drove a vehicle load of teens. Jackie sat in the front passenger seat. She glanced over at her mom, who kept her gaze on the tight curves of the highway leading to the ocean. Mom especially had hovered over her in the last six weeks, relentlessly checking to make sure she hadn't hurt herself. It had only been a couple of weeks since her mom had stopped asking to see Jackie's arms every day.

Dad left the hovering to Mom, but he did hang around more and help Jackie with her homework. After her three-day stay in the hospital, she had a ton of schoolwork to catch up on. One assignment included three poems with artwork. While she painted out in the yard, Dad would run inside and find the colors she needed. Then he'd stay around to give her ideas on what would look cool. He was so into it, and for that little while Jackie actually felt close to him.

The winding highway dipped down toward the beach towns. Jackie's thoughts shifted toward those next few weeks after school. Once classes were over, she attended the diversion program recommended by the hospital—something to help with the communication in the family. She'd gone with her mom every Monday for several weeks.

She'd burned herself on her stomach, a place no one checked. Today, while swimming, she'd have to be careful.

Jackie watched out the window as her mom changed lanes and merged toward another highway. She brushed away a tear. Dad didn't want to come, or couldn't—or something. She wished he had.

She put her hand across her stomach. After a few weeks, the checking up on her had lightened. She'd made it through a month without hurting herself. Then, a few days ago, staying on top of the emotions and pressures got to be too much. The out-of-control anxiety she had felt before returned. She'd burned

SCARS THAT WOUND : SCARS THAT HEAL

herself on her stomach, a place no one checked. Today, while swimming, she'd have to be careful.

The church van and other cars pulled up to the beach, and Jackie spotted the water. It was tradition—she and Melody would spend most of the day hanging out and floating as far out as they could go. She loved the water. With her golden skin tone, Jackie could easily stay out in the water for long periods without burning. The cool Pacific waves were just what she needed on this hot, mid-July day.

Over the next hour, the parents and teens unpacked the food in the picnic area and set up the volleyball net. Once they all ate and cleaned up, the youth group scattered to take walks, play volleyball, or swim.

"Hey Jackie, let's get wet," Melody said as she put away the leftover meat slices in a cooler.

"I'm so ready," Jackie said as she kicked off her flip-flops. Though the cuts on her arms were nearly healed, she'd wait until she got to the water to peel off her hooded shirt. After that she could keep her arms under the water. She wanted everyone to forget what had happened at the retreat.

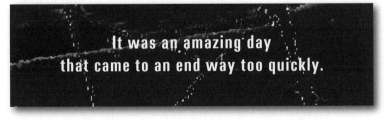

It was an amazing day
that came to an end way too quickly.

Melody and Jackie stayed out almost until dusk. Some of the others swam out to join them, but didn't stay long; they'd return to the shallow waters or to sunning on the beach. One time Melody and Jackie began a wild swim toward shore when they saw sharp fins breaking through the water only fifteen feet away. They stopped and laughed when they realized the fins belonged to a group of dolphins. Melody called the other kids out to watch.

It was an amazing day that came to an end way too quickly.

Everyone swam in and Jackie picked up her shirt, still lying where she had left it. She pulled it on as she walked toward the picnic area.

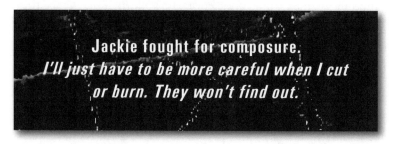

Jackie fought for composure. I'll just have to be more careful when I cut or burn. They won't find out.

Mom spotted her and smiled. "Ready to get changed and head home?"

Jackie nodded. She slipped on her flip-flops and grabbed her bag. When they got to the bathrooms, she washed the salty seawater off her body and then began to change. Her mom was just a few feet away. Tired from the day in the sun and water, she forgot about the marks on her body she had worked so hard to hide.

It was only a moment before she caught the concerned look on Mom's face. "What is that?" she asked, pointing to the four square welts on Jackie's stomach.

Jackie turned away. *Mom, leave me alone.* Her silent plea seemed to work. For now. But she knew Mom wouldn't stop there.

They got home and were heading in the front door when Mom asked again. "Jackie, show me your stomach."

Jackie knew it wasn't worth the fight. Without a word, she lifted up her shirt.

"What are those?" Mom pointed to her stomach. She didn't wait for an answer. "How did you do it?"

"They're burns."

"From what?"

"A lighter."

"What kind of lighter?"

"Barbecue."

"I thought you stopped this, Jackie. This is crazy. This is hurting you." When Jackie didn't respond, she let out an exasperated breath. "What are we going to do with you? Do we need to take you back to the hospital?"

"No," Jackie said firmly. "I don't need to go back."

I won't go back. I can't. The people there don't understand me. No one does.

Jackie fought for composure. *I'll just have to be more careful when I cut or burn. They won't find out.*

Such a large crowd of witnesses is all around us!
So we must get rid of everything that slows us down,
especially the sin that just won't let go. And we must be
determined to run the race that is ahead of us.

Hebrews 12:1 (CEV)

Once in a while, Jackie caught glimpses of hope that life could be more normal for her. More often, reality seemed to steal that hope. "Things weren't changing at home. Nothing changed," she said as she reflected on those next few months after she got out of the hospital. "I was always fighting with my parents and Nikki. My dad was still drinking a lot. He never came in staggering, but I wasn't sure what he'd do when he came home. Most of the time it was his yelling that made me feel unsettled. He'd always yell about the house being a mess, even if it was clean." Her mom and dad's relationship suffered. Jackie's life mirrored the chaos. "I started using harder drugs. It was kind of a mixture of addiction and escape, but definitely escape."

She lost interest in church. "I was starting to check out. I'd show up at youth group just to show up. I still had friends there. I still talked to the adult leaders—just not like I used to."

As Jackie's self-abuse through drugs, sex, and self-injury deepened, many in her church family felt unsure how to help. To Melody, what Jackie was doing seemed like a game being played over and over—doing well for a while, only to eventually trip up. Melody said, "I backed off, feeling I was causing more harm because I was too available to her—like I was perpetuating the situation. I didn't leave. I just wasn't as readily available."

There were others who grew weary and backed off as well. Jackie noticed. "I knew people still cared, but I sensed they didn't know what to do, and I wasn't pushing for them to listen to me as much. I began to pull away."

Jackie finished her junior year and careened recklessly toward her final year of high school. The chaos only multiplied. "Seventeen was a horrible year," Jackie said. "I was out of control with cutting, drugs, sex, and everything. And a lot of bad stuff happened. While walking one day, I hitched a ride from some guys. One of them raped me. I didn't tell anyone. I figured everyone would say it was my fault. Later that year I started hanging out with an older guy and having sex with him. I got pregnant and then miscarried. Everything was a lot worse that year. I just didn't care anymore about anything."

Jackie expressed her despair through images she created on one of her bedroom walls that she had painted black. With a glow-in-the-dark crayon, she wrote curse words. She drew pictures of her thoughts about her molestations and self-injury. The pictures and words hidden during daylight became visible in the dark when she used a black light. It was one more secret expression of the anguish she felt inside.

Jackie attended counseling sessions during this time. Her mom believed she was doing better. "She seemed to be on track, but months into her counseling I could hear it in her answers— it was just a big game," Betty recalled.

Jackie openly shared her lifestyle with her counselor, but they never talked about why she made the choices she did. "I think my counselor thought I was a typical teen in rebellion," she said, looking back. "She wasn't a Christian, so I never got spiritual direction. I pulled away from the church people, and I was talking to a woman who had no concept of God. I was floating around spiritually."

Where did all this leave Jackie? "I felt like I was by myself trying to deal with all this." No matter what her actions seemed to say, she longed for someone to be there, to be honest with her, and not grow weary of her.

> It's natural to want someone who is intentionally hurting herself to just stop. Realize that though that sounds easy to you, it's not to her. Be careful about imposing your timing or agenda. Find ways to continue to support and encourage your friend.

NEVER ALONE

Sometimes in your pain and confusion, you choose to pull away. Sometimes others pull away from you. Either may leave you feeling sad and lonely, maybe even abandoned.

There were many times that Jesus met people who struggled with disease and destructive lifestyles. He never turned away from any of them.

Consider the leper covered in sores and cuts. Others declared him "unclean" and sent him to live away from them— the farther away the better. Jesus met him face-to-face where he was, touched his sores with his hands, and healed him (Luke 5:12, 13).

Think about the woman in John 4 who had made many mistakes in her life. Her community judged her loose lifestyle and turned its back on her. When she went to the well near her home, she heard the sneers and felt the rejection. So she drew her water from a well outside the city walls. Jesus met her there. He offered his grace and compassion. "No one who drinks the water I give will ever be thirsty again. The water I give is like a flowing fountain that gives eternal life" (John 4:14, CEV). After her conversation with Jesus, the woman returned to the village with a changed view of who she was and what her life could become.

Another story tells of a man tormented by spiritual darkness—so people bound him in chains. He was so physically strong, however, that the chains couldn't hold him. He lived among tombs, screaming and slashing himself with stones. The people considered him crazy and stayed far away from him. But Jesus came near and freed him from his torment (Mark 5:1-15).

These stories may seem very different from anything you've experienced—except in coming close to how you've felt ashamed, rejected, or isolated. Each person faced challenging circumstances; each was considered an outcast. Avoided and feared by their own communities, they were left to fend for themselves.

We live in different times, but people still don't always know how to respond to things they don't understand. When the changes they hope for don't happen, they don't know what to do. They may care, but they pull away.

The loneliness or rejection can get mixed in with all the other overwhelming emotions. That may lead to a desire to amp up the self-harming behavior—a response that has eased the pain or felt comfortable in the past. But harming yourself when relationships seem to be hurtful or distant is not your only option.

When you feel misunderstood and on your own, try this: for an hour, a day, or longer, think of the people Jesus met. You're never by yourself. You never have to deal with things on your own. Jesus, whose compassionate and healing hands reached out to each of them, reaches out to you. He understands and will never pull away.

I feel lonely right now, God. Lonely and misunderstood. In the eyes of others, my self-injury is confusing. They think I'm not trying or that I'm not changing fast enough. I've made mistakes yesterday and today, and I probably will tomorrow. You understand. When I'm unsure of what's going on in my life and why I'm doing the things I'm doing, help me begin to trust that you will be there and never pull away. Help me begin to listen for your encouragement. With you, I can get through the next moment and the next day and make better and safer choices for myself. AMEN.

> Blessed is the man who trusts in the Lord and whose trust is the Lord. For he will be like a tree planted by the water, that extends its roots by a stream and will not fear when the heat comes; but its leaves will be green, and it will not be anxious in a year of drought nor cease to yield fruit.
>
> JEREMIAH 17:7, 8

SCARS THAT WOUND : SCARS THAT HEAL

GOING DEEPER

- People don't understand. Nothing is changing. Discouragement. Is any of this a part of your present experience? Describe what's going on.

- Sometimes in our hurt or in trying to protect ourselves, we pull away from people who care about us. We pull away from God. It only hurts more. How can you begin to let those who care back in again?

- It's hard to feel good about even the small steps when others don't see the progress you're making. In what way is God working in your life that you can celebrate and maybe share with someone?

DEEPER STILL

Picture Jesus meeting you where you are. He tells you how much he loves you and that he will stay with you no matter what. Write a poem or story, or sketch, draw, or paint the images that you have about that meeting.

five

I can't explain how heavy my heart feels or how bad it hurts.

—Jackie's Journal

JACKIE SHUFFLED BY THE HIGH SCHOOL POOL and up the ramp leading to Mrs. Shepherd's classroom. There was little life in her steps. The afternoon spring sun soaked her black sweatshirt. Still, she pulled down her sleeves and wrapped the hood tighter around her face. Weariness and sadness—plus the pot she had smoked earlier—made each step heavier.

Mrs. Shepherd's classroom door was wide open, as it often was after school. Jackie stood in the doorway for a moment and watched her child development class teacher working at her desk. Jackie scanned the rest of the room. No other students were there, and the computer was open. *Good.* The English assignment she needed to finish wasn't that important, but hanging around here was more peaceful than anywhere else.

"Hi, Jackie. Come on in."

"I have this English paper I've got to write. Can I use the computer?"

Mrs. Shepherd slid a stack of papers out of a folder as she waved toward that desk. "Sure, that's what it's here for. Go for it."

Jackie dropped her backpack on a nearby desk. She sifted through a pile of papers in her pack, pulled out the assignment page, and sat down in front of the monitor. She stared at the screen.

"Do you need some help getting started?" Mrs. Shepherd offered.

"Yeah, I think so."

"Tell me more about the assignment." Jackie watched her teacher push away from her desk and stand. Jackie always liked her outfits—usually skirts and cute tops. Today her peach-colored shirt showed off her short, light brown, highlighted hair.

"Jackie, I know about the cuts. This isn't the first time I've seen them."

Jackie glanced back at the blank screen. "I'm supposed to write about how Scout, in *To Kill a Mockingbird*, deals with the existence of evil." Jackie pushed the edges of her sleeves toward her elbows and rested her hands on the keyboard. "I didn't really finish reading the book."

Jackie looked up. Her teacher's eyes were focused on her arms. Jackie dropped her head and slid her sleeves down.

Mrs. Shepherd reached out and placed her hand on one sleeve, which now covered Jackie's cuts. "Jackie, I know about the cuts. This isn't the first time I've seen them."

Jackie kept her head down.

"Besides, some of your friends have been concerned."

She shot a look Mrs. Shepherd's way.

"Don't worry. They never said it was you. I figured it out."

"How?"

Mrs. Shepherd hooked a strand of hair behind her ear. "All

those days you've stayed after class through lunch period and slept?"

Jackie nodded.

"I saw the cuts when you laid your head on your arms. Your sleeves pull up."

"What are you going to do?"

Mrs. Shepherd pulled a chair over from a nearby table and sat down. "We have to tell someone. At least the guidance counselor."

Then what? Jackie didn't want to think about anyone else knowing—anyone else judging, or misunderstanding, or asking her to stop when she didn't know how to. And she was afraid to let her parents find out. Afraid to let them down even more. Or make them angry.

"Please just let me talk to you," Jackie begged. Her legs were shaking.

"I'll only tell the guidance counselor for now, OK? See what she suggests." She tilted her head to the side. "But you can keep on coming here anytime you want to talk."

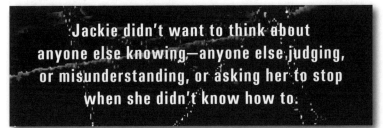

Jackie didn't want to think about anyone else knowing—anyone else judging, or misunderstanding, or asking her to stop when she didn't know how to.

If only talking could fix everything. "OK." Jackie's voice broke.

"You gotta get a handle on this."

Jackie's eyes filled with tears. "I know, but when I feel angry or panicked I don't know what else to do."

"Journal your feelings. When you feel the stress coming on, just start writing. Then write and write and write."

"I can try that." Jackie wiped her cheek and pushed her sweatshirt hood off her head. "I'm really struggling a lot right now. I don't think God is ever going to forgive me for everything I've done."

Mrs. Shepherd stood, went to her desk, and came back with a Bible. "God can forgive anyone. Just ask him. That's who he is. That's what he does." She opened her Bible. "There's a story about a woman who did so many awful things, some of the religious leaders wanted to stone her." She turned the Bible toward Jackie. "Look what Jesus did. He wrote something in the dirt and told those guys that the ones who were without sin could throw the first stone. None could do it. They all left."

Jackie stared at the words in John 8. They seemed like they were for someone else—not her.

> She desired the forgiveness Jesus could give her, but could she let go of the cutting and the drugs that got her through each day?

Her teacher shared more: "Jesus welcomed the woman and that's what he does with you too, Jackie. We're all in this together." Her eyes filled with tears and she squeezed Jackie's hand. "Every one of us needs that kind of forgiveness. We just need to ask him."

Tears suddenly flowed freely from Jackie, but she was also filled with conflict. She desired the forgiveness Jesus could give her, but could she let go of the cutting and the drugs that got her through each day?

It sounded too hard. Way too hard.

The pit felt deep, with walls too sheer and slick to climb out.

> I waited patiently for the Lord; and He inclined to me and heard my cry. He brought me up out of the pit of destruction, out of the miry clay, and He set my feet upon a rock, making my footsteps firm.
>
> PSALM 40:1, 2

ONE TOUGH STEP AT A TIME

By the beginning of her high school senior year, Jackie couldn't scrape together much hope from her life. In her eyes, nothing had changed, nothing made sense. She didn't care anymore. She couldn't. Caring got her nowhere. She was barely putting one foot in front of the other. She was just making it through each day.

Then one of those footsteps took her into Cindy Shepherd's classroom. Cindy had a heart for kids on the fringe. Looking back, Jackie's former teacher said, "The relationship just started developing over the entire year. I was helping her with her homework and trying to encourage her to get to her classes."

As months passed, Jackie discovered she could talk to her teacher. "I wasn't going to Melody as much then, so I think God brought Mrs. Shepherd into my life," she said. Jackie didn't find it easy to trust anyone at that time, but she was willing to give her teacher a chance. "I think it was because she was never pushy. She asked questions but never demanded an answer. And she came across like she was really interested in who I was as opposed to what I was doing." Jackie felt relief that their conversations weren't focused on everything she felt she was doing wrong. "It was more about figuring out what was really going on inside and focusing on that in hopes that it would change my behavior," she said.

Cindy had sensed that Jackie needed someone to lean on, someone who would listen to her. "There were times that she would start talking and she'd ramble," her former teacher said. "I remember thinking that sometimes she was going for shock value. She'd look at me and see if I'd react, maybe checking to see if I'd turn away from her. I'd just laugh and say, 'You know what? You're stuck with me.'"

Cindy knew that Jackie was showing up at school high on drugs most of the time, but it took a while for her to find out about the cutting and burning. When she noticed the marks and then later talked with Jackie, she treaded carefully. "I accepted her for who she was. I didn't overreact about the cutting and problems she was having. I think her confiding was a crucial step for her. She found someone who she could begin to trust, who she could talk to, who would listen to her and wouldn't judge her." Cindy felt Jackie had a lot going on that caused her to want to hurt herself. Her young friend was worth going every extra mile for—she would do what it took to help Jackie discover those deeper things going on inside.

Over the months, Jackie's teacher encouraged her to keep trusting that God would help her. In their conversations, Jackie told her she still loved God and wanted to be in church, but she felt hypocritical. Cindy urged her to stay in church and keep talking to Melody. Jackie did.

A few weeks after she graduated from high school, Jackie received a letter from Melody. It challenged her choices and pleaded with her to get help. Her youth pastor also recommended a ministry for at-risk youth. Jackie felt Melody's concern and knew she was right. She was in trouble.

God was there, helping her take one step at a time, and he sent people to care and walk alongside Jackie. He would continue to be with her in the next stage of her journey.

> Ask the person who is self-injuring to tell you how it all started and, if it's not too hard for her, ask what thoughts and feelings were connected with that decision. Beginning to talk it through and trusting someone to listen without judgment can be a huge step. Ask God to help you respond with wisdom. Realize that it's scary for someone who has been self-harming to think of living without that choice.

SOMEONE TRUSTWORTHY

Finding people who will listen and who you can trust isn't as easy or straightforward as it sounds. Sometimes it feels easier to go online and chat with people who will never really know you. Depending on the various sites out there that you might go to, the information and contacts aren't always safe or helpful, and the result can be a more intensified desire to self-harm. Counselor Christian Hill has seen online opportunities for talking about self-injury actually promote making that choice or even encourage experimentation. "Personal blogs, forums, and chats have allowed teens to speak more openly about self-injury, but it also gives other teens the idea," he said.

Looking back from the vantage point of today, Jackie shares a few tips that might help you find a good person to talk with face-to-face: "Find someone who you're comfortable with and who has your best interest in mind. The person could be someone you already have a relationship with—someone who knows a little about your situation but isn't necessarily involved. Some kids would tell their mom or their friend. That's OK. I always looked for someone outside my family." It's also important, she said, to find a person who has a strong faith in God.

Cindy Shepherd believes that many continue to cut because they can't find someone they feel they can trust. "They've been let down by adults, and so sometimes they're afraid to go to an adult," she said.

But Cindy also has watched the young friends of people who self-injure become overwhelmed. "A lot of kids don't have any clue how to deal with self-injury. It scares them and they want to back off," she said. "Kids are true to their friend, but it doesn't mean they can handle it."

Cindy respects Jackie's feeling on finding friends, and she realizes that not every home situation is the best, but she feels that whenever possible parents should be involved. "I always encourage kids, 'Even though you don't think your parents are with you, they do love you,'" Cindy said. "'You need to get them involved in what you're going through.'"

Kyle found support in his friends, his church family, and especially a couple he adopted as parents. All of them "helped me find the inner strength to seek the help I needed and to bring me back to church, where the biggest part of my journey began. It was with their love, support, listening ears, and constant prayers that I was able to start making changes."

Callie was fortunate to have the encouragement of her parents. "My mom dropped out of her classes to stay with me constantly and take me to my counseling and doctor appointments," she said. "My dad would take me for late-night drives when my anxiety was overwhelming or when I was struggling with wanting to self-injure."

Mari found that her biggest supporters were her counselors. "Being accepted as I am, where I am, is very freeing," she said. They helped her understand more about why she self-injured and offered alternate behaviors. She also had a best friend who self-injured. "Just being able to talk with someone who's going through the same issues is good. We work together to try to keep from self-injuring."

Counselor Susan Cook suggests connecting with those who have some wisdom and life experience with their own pain. A safe person, she says, is "someone who can handle your pain, who will accept that the pain is real, and is not going to get tripped up in whether the pain seems 'accurate' to them."

You have more options than you may feel right now. The key is to choose people who, as Jackie said, have your best interest in mind.

Here's advice from someone who used to self-injure to those who might want to reach out and help: "Be a true, godly mentor. If you haven't given it all to God, then how can you expect them to? Work on yourself too." The more your friend sees sincere efforts in you, the more they'll be inspired to seek true change.

A Few Good Cot-Bearers

If you've bought into the secretive nature of self-injury, you might find that you're left without the support you desperately need. God designed people to be in relationships, not only with him, but also with others. It's often within relationships, not in isolation, that he does his most awesome healing work. He enjoys sending "Mrs. Shepherds" into situations like yours.

The Bible tells a story about a man who was paralyzed (Luke 5:17-20). When Jesus came to town and visited the house of one his friends, many crowded in the house and surrounding yard to listen to his teaching or to be healed. The paralyzed man wanted to go too, but couldn't get there without help, of course. He had four good friends who were determined to help him. They laid him on a cot, lifted him up, and took him to the house where Jesus was.

When they got there, they realized the crowds made it nearly impossible to get anywhere near Jesus. But those guys didn't give up. They knew how the houses were built. Some believe they used ropes to work like a pulley to hoist the man on the cot up to the roof. This we do know for sure: after removing

SCARS THAT WOUND : SCARS THAT HEAL

a few roof tiles, they lowered their friend right in front of Jesus. Can't you picture Jesus' smile? Luke 5:20 says, "Seeing their faith, He said, 'Friend, your sins are forgiven you.'" Jesus recognized not only the faith of the man on the cot but his friends' faith too. They showed their faith through determined, creative action to help the man get close to Jesus.

That's the kind of friend and support person you want to have around. When you're feeling too weary or hopeless to take the next step, look for a few trustworthy people who might be willing to be cot-bearers. Look for someone who will do whatever it takes to get you closer to Jesus.

God, in a lot of ways I have kept my self-injury to myself. I haven't wanted to let others in. Sometimes I've turned to people I don't know or people who haven't been that good for me. Make me aware of the kinds of situations that won't bring me closer to you or to the healing you have in mind for me. Help me look for people who will honor who I am and your plan for me, who will be honest and supportive even when they don't fully understand. AMEN.

> **So you will walk in the way of good men
> and keep to the paths of the righteous.**
> PROVERBS 2:20

■ Secrets and fears can keep you from having those really solid, face-to-face relationships that God wants to give you to help you heal and grow. Are there any secrets you are holding on to?

■ Do you spend time with people who aren't interested in honoring who God created you to be, or his plan for you? What's one thing you can do differently to be sure that you can continue to heal and grow?

■ How can you adjust your expectations of others so you can let them care about you in the best way they can and allow them to move you closer to Jesus?

DEEPER STILL

Create a "possibility list" of people who are not only good support people for you but also who know Jesus well. Choose one or two. Ask them if they will help you grow closer to God. Be humble. Be willing to listen and learn.

six

The truth is, I know God is constantly embracing me.
I pray one day I truly feel that.

—Jackie's Journal

"ARE YOU LISTENING?"

"Yes, I'm listening."

"Really?"

Jackie laughed and assured her new friend, Sue, for about the hundredth time that she was really listening.

"Yes, really."

"Thanks. People usually don't." Sue smiled as she pulled her long blond hair back and clipped it up.

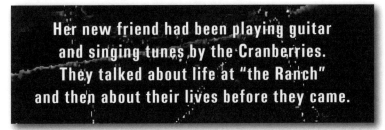

Her new friend had been playing guitar and singing tunes by the Cranberries. They talked about life at "the Ranch" and then about their lives before they came.

For the previous three hours the two girls had been sitting outside on an upper deck of the lodge at a residential ministry for at-risk youth. Jackie arrived just a few weeks before, after Melody had urged her to consider applying to the ministry so she could get help. Jackie was accepted and moved in by the middle of summer. She missed her family, but at least she was getting to know some of the people here.

Like Sue. The two of them seemed to end up on the back deck a lot—just hanging out. Tonight her new friend had been playing guitar and singing tunes by the Cranberries. They talked about life at "the Ranch" and then about their lives before they came.

> Should she tell Sue about her cutting?
> She seemed easy to talk to.

Sue glanced toward the dining room windows. "I can't believe they're letting us stay out here for so long." She shrugged. "But I'm glad. I've never told anybody what I just told you."

"Serious?"

Sue nodded. "Maybe some of it, but no one has really listened like you did. And I can tell you won't tell others."

Jackie smiled and scooted her chair back. "I don't repeat stuff. Thanks for trusting me."

They both stood and walked into the lodge dining room. One of the college interns met them. "Hey, you two might want to think about hanging out with some of the others too," she said.

Jackie kept quiet.

Sue spoke up. "We had a good talk. We were helping each other."

The next night they were out on the back deck again, their heads bent over letters they each were writing to family and friends.

SCARS THAT WOUND : SCARS THAT HEAL

Jackie stopped and looked up. Should she tell Sue about her cutting? She seemed easy to talk to.

Jackie started writing again, but then put her pen down. She'd just go for it. "You know, Sue, people here don't know this yet, but part of the reason why I came is because I cut myself."

Sue looked puzzled. "What do you mean?"

"I mean I hurt myself on purpose. When I get really angry or anxious or when things are really hard for me emotionally, I cut or burn myself."

"I've never heard of that." Sue seemed to be considering what to say next. "I guess I sort of take out my emotional pain on myself too. I do it through eating a lot and throwing up."

"Really?"

Sue nodded. "I started doing it when I began to feel too much pressure about how I looked or what I was doing. A lot of times I did it when things felt out of control with my family. When I feel angry or anxious, I eat way beyond even stuffing myself. So I throw up."

"Yeah?"

"Yeah. I can hide it most of the time."

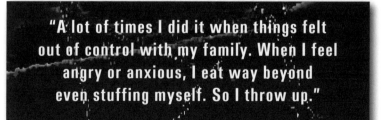

"A lot of times I did it when things felt out of control with my family. When I feel angry or anxious, I eat way beyond even stuffing myself. So I throw up."

"Same with my cutting. I know I need help. I'm here for more than the partying I was doing, but that's the reason the other kids think I'm here."

An intern leaned out the door. "Hey guys. It's time to head up to the dorms."

Sue and Jackie gathered up their letters and pens and dropped them off in their storage cubbies just inside the door.

Sue turned toward Jackie. "Hey, thanks for sharing."

"Yeah, you too."

> Sue pushed her hands into her dark blue sweatshirt and turned toward Jackie. "I think we can help each other. Your cutting and my eating problems—they're what we go to in our darkest moments."

Together they walked through the kitchen, headed outside, and climbed the seventy-eight cement steps that wound their way through the overhanging trees. Residents like Jackie and Sue made this walk to their dorms several times each day. Counting the irregular, rock-lined steps placed into the hillside at least gave the bored mind something to do.

As they split off in the hallway to go to their separate rooms, Sue said, "You know, Jackie, we really should pray about your cutting and my overeating."

"Yeah, we should sometime."

"How about now?" Sue paused and looked toward the doors. "I can ask."

Jackie nodded.

Sue went to each room and convinced the intern leaders to let them sit outside the dorm for a few minutes of prayer.

The warm August night was filled with the sounds of bullfrogs and crickets. One small lamp lit the steps where Jackie and Sue sat down to pray.

Sue pushed her hands into her dark blue sweatshirt and turned toward Jackie. "I think we can help each other. Your cutting and my eating problems—they're what we go to in our darkest moments. Maybe we can figure out a better way to deal with things."

"Yeah, I really need this prayer," Jackie said. "I want to stop cutting. I don't know why I do it. Or why I keep doing it."

Sue looked back toward the door. "They're not going to let us stay out here long. I'll start." They bowed their heads, and Sue began. "Lord, I pray for Jackie, that you would free her from her cutting. Let the right people into her life who can help her . . ."

"God," Jackie prayed a short time later, "give Sue strength to do something different with her emotions than throwing up. Give us strength to find different ways to deal with our problems . . ."

Therefore, confess your sins to one another, and
pray for one another so that you may be healed.
The effective prayer of a righteous man can accomplish much.

JAMES 5:16

Two very different roads lay before Jackie. One seemed to offer possibilities for a better future, while the other looked treacherous and dark. The residential ministry everyone called "the Ranch" seemed like her best hope. "I felt that if something didn't happen with that, I wasn't going to make it in life," Jackie remembered. "I would either die by suicide or a drug overdose. I felt like it was a life-or-death situation."

The letter Melody wrote helped Jackie see she needed a lot more help than she was getting. Her parents weren't as easy to convince. They wanted her to be OK. She wasn't. "I talked to my mom, and she just said that I needed to get a job. My dad said the same thing—that if I'd just do something with my life, I wouldn't do that stuff anymore."

Betty, Jackie's mom, hoped for normalcy. "I remember thinking, 'We have ups and downs and we move on. Get a job, sign up for college, and continue on.' Melody definitely knew Jackie needed more."

To try to get her parents to understand, Jackie showed her mom drawings and song lyrics that focused on hating life and dying. "I recall Jackie showing me those things, and it was just numbing," Betty remembered. "Like, who would ever write or draw or think this way? Why does Jackie think this way? It was still the same question: Why?"

While her mom and dad were trying to grasp the depth of her struggles, Jackie pursued finding out what it would take to get into the residential ministry. She received the information by mail, and Melody helped her fill out an application. By midsummer, after her high school graduation, her parents finally agreed. They drove Jackie on the two-hour trip to the Ranch.

It was a hard move for Jackie. She cared deeply for her family and knew she would miss them, even with the problems at home. She had begun to blame herself for more of those issues. She hoped that by getting help, things would be better for everyone. "I believed everything was my fault and I caused my own pain," Jackie said. "If I could fix me, then I could fix my family, and there wouldn't be so much chaos."

"Fixing" wouldn't come easily, as Jackie found out. "The first time I cut myself at the Ranch I felt really hopeless because I just didn't understand. I thought once I went there I was going to get counseling, and I was going to get better quickly."

And God's part of the process? In one sense, Jackie felt confident that she had a relationship with him. But she lived with plenty of uncertainties at the same time. "I wasn't sure if he *wanted* to help me or, if he did, how he would help me."

With her friendship with Sue and others at the Ranch, Jackie began to grasp that she mattered to God. "Praying with Sue was a big step in knowing he cared. Everyone's kindness really opened up my eyes to God's love for me. He was blessing me with more people who could help."

Sue had never been close to anyone who had self-injured, but she remembered wanting to be a supportive friend for Jackie. "I thought, 'This is bigger than me,'" Sue said. "'I don't understand it.' So I wanted to get prayer into the situation. I couldn't be her emotional support, but I could be her prayer buddy."

Sue understood self-injury more than she thought. Her own self-harming behavior, her eating disorder, came from the pressure she felt from her mother to lose weight. A friend facing the same pressure taught her how to purge. Sue was ripe for this temptation. "I wasn't feeling accepted for how I looked. I had other emotional roots in that. It started as a weight issue and became a control issue. Things around me were out of control. I didn't know how to deal with anger or anxiety, and I'd eat and eat. Way beyond just stuffing myself. Then I'd throw up."

What these two young women had in common launched their friendship, but even more important to Jackie was Sue's insisting that prayer be a part of their accountability. "I was thankful that we were comfortable with each other and that she suggested praying," Jackie recalled. "I remember thinking that I really admired her for that."

Said Sue, "In my mind I felt confident that the Lord could heal her of this." Besides praying for her friend, Sue enjoyed lightening the mood for Jackie. "We had a lot of fun together— laughed a lot, acted crazy. I'd tell the others, 'Let's grab some brooms, make 'em batons, march in there like a school band, and give Jackie a show.' We knew she'd want to laugh. You can handle the serious things if things aren't always heavy."

With the beginnings of a friendship rooted in prayer, Jackie began to trust God a little more. "I felt at that point I was letting God be more a part of my cutting," she said. "I don't think I had really thought to pray to stop cutting—to honestly ask him."

It would be some time, however, before Jackie understood and fully took that step. Some horrible struggles were still ahead of her. But God kept meeting her where she was and bringing people into her life to add encouragement or accountability.

If you're helping someone who self-injures, ask him about his triggers—places, events, times, or things that move him to the point of wanting to hurt himself. Make sure he knows he can call on you if he needs help through a difficult time. Make sure he has others available as well so there is always someone there for him if you're not around.

WORKING OUT ACCOUNTABILITY

Jackie found strong friendships and support in people such as Melody, Mrs. Shepherd, and Sue, all of whom God had brought into her life. They listened to her, cried with her, prayed for her, and never stopped hoping she'd find a way to heal and find enjoyment in the life God had planned for her. Others have found similar support.

Callie had a friend she felt she could tell anything and know that friend would stick by her. "Sometimes I'd be IM-ing with her and tell her I was having a hard time," Callie said. "She'd say she had to go and she'd talk to me later. Five minutes would go by, she'd be at my door saying, 'Come on. You're going shopping with me.' This happened a bunch of times. I'd be in a rough spot, and she'd help me break out of my cycle." Callie's friend also was willing to be honest with her. "She wasn't afraid to tell me things straight up," Callie said.

Carrie and her friend support each other in quitting their self-injury. "We talk to each other at least once a week and help each other when relapses occur," Carrie said. "When we've gone so long without it, we reward each other and encourage each other to continue the hard work."

Ryan regularly talked to others who self-injured. "It made me feel loved and supported," he recalled. Not everyone is the best choice to tell the deepest stuff to, though. Looking back, Ryan realized it didn't work so well when he made his girlfriend one of those he confided in. "I saw how it hurt her," he said.

Jordan found a friend in his youth group. "A guy from the group talked to me, and I felt like God gave me more hope," Jordan said.

Realistically, support people can't always be available when you need them, and they won't do everything right. Jordan battled with wanting to cut himself one night; he couldn't get in touch with any of his accountability partners. "They were busy with their own lives," he said.

Dan admitted that knowing he is going to meet with someone next week isn't enough to keep him from hurting himself today. It helps, he said, when people regularly ask him how things are going. "That gives me an opportunity to share more about it and work through the feelings I have about it."

Having the right amount of both accountability and support are intangibles you have to work out. You know your triggers and problem times. You know what helps. Never give up. Keep communicating. What you're experiencing is important enough to share with others. Counselor Susan Cook, who has met with lots of teens and young adults who self-injure, says that just feeling valued and connected with others may begin to solve some things for you.

And be aware of when the support you have isn't enough. Don't hesitate to ask your pastor, or someone else who might know, about the resources or ministries in your community. Sometimes, as in Jackie's case, it becomes a matter of what's best for your life and health. Get the help you need to make sure you're safe.

> Ask the person you're encouraging what kind of support plan will work best. Consider whether regular meetings are helpful, if phone calls are needed, or both. Help her find ways to express herself and to discover the strengths and gifts God has given her. Be as available as is realistic for your life. Include prayer in the times you spend together. Go deep. Like Sue, be open about your struggles and needs as well.

GOING FOR IT

When someone comes alongside to hold you accountable, and they include God in the equation, you've got an amazing tool in your hands—one more powerful than the tool you use to hurt yourself. But even more powerful than that is when you're willing to fully allow and even actively pursue the difference that support can make.

The Bible tells about a man named Bartimaeus who was blind and poor (Matthew 20:29-34; Mark 10:46-52; Luke 18:35-43). Every day he and a friend sat by a dusty street to beg. One day Jesus was passing by. It didn't matter to Bartimaeus that he couldn't see Jesus. It didn't matter that it seemed nearly impossible to shout through the gathering crowds to ask for his help. When he did yell his request, some told him to be quiet. That didn't matter either. Bartimaeus wanted healing that bad. And if he was going to get it, he needed to do something about it.

A lot happened in the next few moments of this story.

First, Jesus asked others to bring the man to him.

Family, friends, accountability partners, pastors, counselors.

Then Jesus asked what Bartimaeus wanted him to do for him. Bartimaeus told him he wanted to get well; he wanted to see.

God, I want to live differently. I believe you can make me well.

Jesus saw his faith and told Bartimaeus he was well. *Well* in different versions of the Bible might read as *whole, healed,* or *saved.* Here's a quick lesson in Greek, in which the New Testament was written: The word used in this story for *well* is *sozo,* which means "protected" and "delivered from danger or destruction." Jesus healed Bartimaeus's blindness, but also spiritually saved him from destruction.

You can be like Bartimaeus by recognizing your need and not letting anything stop you from pursuing your healing. Look at what you are able to do right now to let others help you get up off the side of your road. As they come alongside and take you closer to Jesus, be bold in answering his question: "What do you want?" Ask him to heal you and help you.

God, I sit on the side of the road of my life in need of your healing. It can get pretty comfortable here sometimes. Help me to see my need clearly and to fully want your healing. All the accountability

partners in the world won't mean a thing if I don't
want to be made well—physically and spiritually.
You're here on the road in front of me and asking
what I want. Jesus, please heal me. AMEN.

> Jesus said to him, "Receive your sight; your faith
> has made you well." Immediately he regained his sight
> and began following Him, glorifying God;
> and when all the people saw it, they gave praise to God.
>
> LUKE 18:42, 43

GOING DEEPER

■ Though he was blind, Bartimaeus used the resources available to him to pursue his healing. What are the strengths and resources you can use today?

■ Your willingness to face the hurts in your life so you can overcome self-injury is the first key in any accountability relationship. What are you willing to commit to doing differently, starting today, that God can use in such a relationship?

■ List as many ways as you can think of that people experience being made well by Jesus. Which ones would you like to experience?

DEEPER STILL

A journaling exercise: Imagine yourself sitting on the side of a road like Bartimaeus, and you don't want to stay there one day longer. Who is around you who can help you get up from your spot beside the road? What resources are right there on the street by which you're sitting? When Jesus comes your way, what will you do? Write your honest reflections before God.

seven

Yesterday Mike prayed with me and the topic was my cutting on myself. It was really good. So much was said.

—Jackie's Journal

JACKIE HELPED FINISH THE MORNING DISHES, but her mind was somewhere else. Today she would meet with Mike, the director of the ministry, but also a counselor. John, her usual counselor, was out of town. She was nervous. It wasn't that Mike was intimidating. Yeah, his six-foot-plus frame towered over her, but he seemed nice, always encouraging others in his quiet, caring way. She just didn't know him. Jackie had seen him around but usually didn't say much to him—only smiled, said hi, and went on.

> She kept the sleeves of her sweatshirt anchored in her hands. She longed for freedom from the deep pain she felt inside and the guilt she carried from years of abuse.

She scrubbed the counters, waiting. Then he was there in the kitchen, chatting with some of the other girls. He turned her way. "Hi, Jackie. Ready to come down to my office?"

Jackie smiled and hid her nervousness behind her deep dimples. "Yeah, sure."

She followed him through the Ranch living room and down the stairs to his office. Mike's desk sat against the wall at one end of the narrow room; a window overlooked a pond at the other end. A bookshelf and black vinyl couch lined one wall. As Mike settled into his desk chair, Jackie shuffled past him toward the couch. She thought carefully about where she'd sit, then chose the middle cushion. From there, she could keep her distance, and it wouldn't be too noticeable.

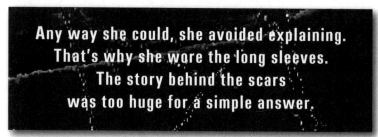

Any way she could, she avoided explaining. That's why she wore the long sleeves. The story behind the scars was too huge for a simple answer.

The office was warm. It was a ninety-degree August day. The fan on top of the bookshelf whirred quietly, barely moving the stifling air. Jackie tugged at the sleeves of her black sweatshirt and gripped the edges tightly in her fists.

As Mike swiveled his chair toward her and stretched his long legs, she wondered where this meeting would go. They began to chat casually about her friends and family back home and then about how things were going at the ministry. What did she think about the upcoming wilderness trip? Was she OK with it? Yeah, that wasn't a problem. Jackie began to feel more at ease.

Then Mike turned the conversation in a more personal direction. "It's a pretty big step to come here to the Ranch. Tell me what led you to make that decision."

SCARS THAT WOUND : SCARS THAT HEAL

"Well . . ." Jackie really didn't know where to begin, but gave it a try. "It was Melody's idea. I guess—I guess I was messing up, using drugs and alcohol." She hesitated. "And I hurt myself—like I cut and burned myself." She put it past tense. It sounded better.

"How are you doing with hurting yourself now—here?" Mike asked.

"Yeah, I've done it here." She didn't say how recently.

The next few moments Mike patiently asked her questions. Jackie remained mostly quiet but told more of her story—almost all in one-sentence answers. She kept the sleeves of her sweatshirt anchored in her hands. She longed for freedom from the deep pain she felt inside and the guilt she carried from years of abuse. Though their meeting was about over, Mike seemed to pick up on her need for something more.

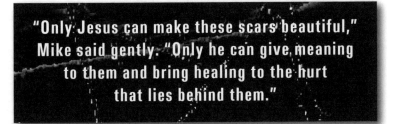

"Only Jesus can make these scars beautiful," Mike said gently. "Only he can give meaning to them and bring healing to the hurt that lies behind them."

"Before we finish up, I want to pray and bring all of this to Jesus," he said. Mike paused. "Would you be willing to pull back your sleeves so we can bring your scars to him?"

Jackie's anxiety shot up. No one had ever asked her to reveal her scars, and there were many. They made her feel ugly; she hated everything about them. She didn't like the questions and the stares. Any way she could, she avoided explaining.

That's why she wore the long sleeves. The story behind the scars was too huge for a simple answer.

And yet she had just shared part of that story with Mike. Could she let *him* see the scars?

She looked at Mike. She could tell he wasn't asking out of curiosity, like she was part of some freak show. He genuinely cared. Slowly, she slid up both sleeves to reveal forearms slashed with many marks, some of them fresh.

"Jackie, only Jesus can make these scars beautiful," Mike said gently. "Only he can give meaning to them and bring healing to the hurt that lies behind them. Can we pray for that?"

Jackie looked down at her scars. *Make* these *beautiful?* It sounded crazy.

"Jesus came to save the lost. His blood-stained hands, feet, and side are proof of the death-defying power of his love for us," Mike said. "There is no place his love cannot reach."

She wanted to believe that.

> Jackie felt Mike's light touch on her arms
> as he prayed that she would believe
> that Christ's blood was sufficient
> to heal every area of her life.

He went on. "Jesus told Thomas to put his hands in his side, to see the wounds in his hands. The wounds of Christ built unshakable confidence in Thomas's heart. His doubts were put to rest as he touched the most beautiful of scars."

Jackie searched Mike's eyes. *Can God really do that? Use my scars and cuts in a beautiful way?*

Mike answered her silent questions. "We can pray that Jesus' wounds and scars be the healing of yours. Can I pray for that for you?"

He wasn't pushing. Jackie could tell she could say no and he'd be OK with it, but she always seemed to struggle with pleasing everyone. Tears burned her eyes. She partly wanted to say yes so she wouldn't seem ungrateful for his help. Mostly, she craved the healing he talked about. She nodded. They bowed their heads.

"Jesus, make your wounds Jackie's wounds. Make Jackie's wounds full of purpose and meaning, without fear of guilt." Jackie felt Mike's light touch on her arms as he prayed that she would believe that Christ's blood was sufficient to heal every area of her life. He asked that the scars she hid would become reminders of Jesus' love for her in the days ahead.

He finished and they lifted their heads. Tears streaked both their faces.

"Jackie, it took great courage to share your scars. Thank you for revealing your pain and letting me pray for you."

She left Mike's office that day with a smile she couldn't hold back. She realized the step she had taken and what it meant. It was a beginning she thought she'd never see. For the first time, she felt a sliver of hope. Jesus' wounds and scars were for her, and they held the promise that hers would be healed. Maybe hers too could become beautiful scars.

Was that really possible? Could she get better and overcome the urges to hurt herself?

seven

> A woman who had hemorrhaged for twelve years slipped in
> from behind and lightly touched his robe. She was thinking to
> herself, "If I can just put a finger on his robe, I'll get well." Jesus
> turned—caught her at it. Then he reassured her: "Courage,
> daughter. You took a risk of faith, and now you're well."
>
> MATTHEW 9:20, 21 (THE MESSAGE)

MY WOUNDS AND SCARS

But even as Jackie voluntarily sought help, self-injury kept a strong hold on her.

She couldn't figure it out: *Why am I doing this? Am I crazy? Will I ever stop? Could it get worse?* Her mom had wondered too. "I didn't think I'd see Jackie reach her eighteenth birthday," Betty said.

Even Jackie was beginning to wonder if she'd make it to adulthood. Mike was aware of this and was deeply concerned. He didn't want to waste any opportunity. "I knew about Jackie's depression and her conviction that there was no way out of her compulsion to hurt herself," he said. He remembered that her eyes were full of conflicting emotions—hurt, sadness, and distrust—and yet also pleading for help. He felt an urgency to bring her self-injury out into the open.

Jackie didn't understand how intertwined her emotions and memories were with her self-injury. "I desperately wanted to figure out why I cut. I really didn't know," she recalled. At the time, she still battled between longing to tell her story and being afraid of the consequences. Though she was experiencing real connections and support, Jackie carried leftover hurts and fears from those times when letting others in hadn't worked so well. "Everything was getting complicated. It was causing problems for everyone," she said. This was one of the deepest feelings she wrestled with. She also struggled with the fear of betraying her family, getting teased for being overly sensitive (her family would do that at times), or wearing out more support people. She thought those at the Ranch might not be able to help her. *Are they going to get tired of me too?* she wondered.

During the first two months at the Ranch, Jackie's counseling sessions with John and his willingness to be available to the max laid the groundwork for her to begin to trust again. And then came the day Mike invited her into his office.

Of his request for Jackie to lift up her sleeves, Mike said, "I was stupidly bold to ask her to let me see her scars." He knew that not many who self-injure are quickly open to that kind of vulnerability. Looking back today, both Mike and Jackie know God was powerfully at work.

> How someone sees his scars may be very close to how he sees himself as a person: "They're ugly; I'm ugly and worthless." Keep that in mind as you talk to him. Be sensitive and caring in your choice of words.

The story about Jesus' scars and the revelation that he could make Jackie's scars beautiful made an impact. "That never crossed my mind (before)," Jackie said, looking back. "I felt so negative and depressed. Just the fact that someone looked at it differently gave me that smile I couldn't wipe off my face. Before that day the prayers were always 'Jesus, heal Jackie because she is so screwed up.' This didn't feel that way to me. Jesus really cared." She paused. "Mike said 'without fear of guilt'—I was full of guilt, and that changed my perspective of Jesus' view of me."

Jackie still battled urges to hurt herself, and she gave in at times, but she had the beginnings of the hope that God wouldn't give up on her. Today she encourages others who self-harm that "the most important thing for me is the love Jesus has for me no matter what. He does care about our emotional stuff. It makes him sad that we feel we have to hurt ourselves because we are in so much pain."

Jackie courageously shared her scars. New beginnings often involve risks: trusting someone, trusting Jesus.

It can be difficult for someone who self-injures to trust others and take the steps needed to get help. When she does, tell her that you recognize the courage it took.

JESUS' SCARS THAT HEAL

Jackie's scars and wounds were powerful representations of her deep emotions. Likely, so are yours. Each injury may symbolize a desire for independence, control, or other extremely personal and intense feelings. It can be a struggle to stop even if the scars feel ugly or cause shame. The act of hurting oneself can feel like a best friend who listens and cares and doesn't grow tired of you.

But as Jackie discovered, there is a better friend—someone who understands scars and wounds, someone who will listen and care and never become weary of fighting for your life and heart.

"See my scars" was the essential message that the resurrected Jesus said to Thomas on first appearing to him (John 20:27). Scars packed with meaning. Jesus had come to earth and put on human skin to live, breathe, feel, and hurt like you and I do. He had crazy expectations thrown at him. He was spat on, misrepresented, and betrayed—sometimes by those he was closest to.

He then endured humiliation and whippings, a crown of thorns pressed onto his head, a heavy cross placed on his shoulders, and nails hammered into his wrists and feet. So many wounds you couldn't count them. But each welt, gash, and bruise on Jesus' body shouts "I love you" and, if accepted, is a gift of freedom and healing.

His scars and wounds given in exchange for yours.

Only Jesus, as God come to earth, had the power to bear scars that have the ability to reach deep into the hearts of people and heal the hidden pain they feel inside. That's why another cut or another burn or another punch to a wall isn't enough. "Another" is never enough. But the wounds Jesus bore are. As he took his last breath on the cross, he said, "It is finished" (John 19:30). Wrapped up in those words is the power of his wounds—Jesus' completion of God's plan to set right each person's messed-up relationship with him and to make it possible for them to experience the depth of his love.

After Jesus told Thomas to look at his scars, he then said, "Believe."

See his scars. See what they mean. Believe. As Mike told Jackie, Christ's shed blood is sufficient to heal every area of your life. As Jesus helps you overcome the urges to hurt yourself, allow your fading scars—those on the inside as well as the outside—to become reminders of his love for you. You'll be witnessing an amazing and powerful expression of the most beautiful of scars—Jesus' scars that heal.

Jesus, as I think about the reasons why I hurt myself, help me grab onto the meaning of your beautiful scars—scars that heal. Mine keep me stuck in my pain, but yours bring freedom. My scars tell me to do it again, but yours say "It's done." The love behind each of your wounds takes away all my pain, guilt, and shame. Sometimes that's hard to believe. Help me believe. And when I feel like hurting myself when everything seems so hard, remind me again. Thank you that you are here and will never leave me. AMEN.

> **It was for freedom that Christ set us free; therefore keep standing firm and do not be subject again to a yoke of slavery.**
> GALATIANS 5:1

SCARS THAT WOUND : SCARS THAT HEAL

GOING DEEPER

■ Jesus understands your scars and wounds—those on the inside as well as the outside. Take a look again at his scars and wounds. Ask this question: What do they mean for me?

■ In thinking about what Jesus willingly went through for you personally, do you hear his message of "I love you"? What does that message mean for your self-injury? What else might he be saying to you about your pattern of self-harm?

■ Jesus showed Thomas his scars and then said, "Believe." At a deeper level, what was Jesus asking Thomas to do? When he shows you his scars and says the same thing to you, what is he asking you to believe?

DEEPER STILL

Write a letter to Jesus telling him how you picture his healing of your inner scars. Include what your life would look like if you had that healing. Decide on a step you're willing to take to begin to bring that healing about—and then tell Jesus. Pray and ask for his help as you take that step.

eight

The past two nights I've been feeling fearful.
It's a different kind than I'm used to.
I want to cry but the tears won't come.

—Jackie's Journal

JACKIE WOKE UP BREATHING HARD. Sweating. Someone was there who shouldn't be. He was coming closer. Her eyes shot open. She didn't want his horrible hands on her, his breath near her face. Frozen in place, she peered into the dark. *Stay quiet.* She blinked. Her chest heaved in fear.

Lying on her side facing the wall, she began to recognize the shadowed shapes of greeting cards on her bulletin board. She slowly turned her head. The outline of the door and the other three beds with her sleeping roommates confirmed where she was—in the dorm room at the Ranch.

She was safe.

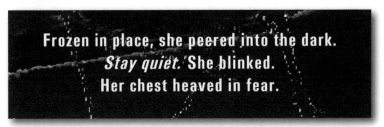

Frozen in place, she peered into the dark.
Stay quiet. She blinked.
Her chest heaved in fear.

Her heart was still beating heavy, hard. She writhed in her covers and then sat up. Dropping her legs over the side of the bed, she opened the top drawer of the nearby dresser. Feeling around among the rolled-up socks, she searched until her fingers found the sharp metal object she sought. Quietly, she lifted her T-shirt and slid the blade across her stomach.

Her breathing slowed and she shut her eyes again. Holding her hand on the new cut, she lay back down and coiled into a ball on her right side, this time facing her roommates. The fear began to fall away. She willed herself to think about anything but the dream. *The work program. Laughing with friends like Sue. The encouraging note Melody had sent.* She reclaimed her sleepy escape.

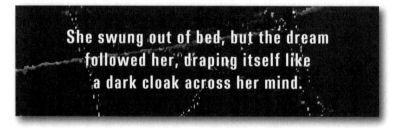

She swung out of bed, but the dream followed her, draping itself like a dark cloak across her mind.

Too soon her alarm clock's beeping pierced her sleep, and she stirred and then stretched. Then she remembered. The dream—it had come again. The more it invaded her sleep the more real it seemed. Was it a reminder of being molested as a child? Maybe just thoughts stirred from recent counseling sessions? This dream seemed different. It introduced a new face—one she once trusted. She curled back into her covers. She was shaking. Was it that cold on this spring morning?

"Come on, Jackie, get up. Breakfast is in five minutes."

She swung out of bed, but the dream followed her, draping itself like a dark cloak across her mind. After breakfast, she tried to push the images away with the busyness of the morning chores. Instead, the dream clung. It menaced.

SCARS THAT WOUND : SCARS THAT HEAL

The Friday afternoon schedule included a "fun day"—an outing for all the residents to a local putt-putt park. But "fun" wasn't how she'd describe this day—not in a million years. No golf or arcade game or go-cart race would shake the clutches of that dream.

At the park, those in her group were breaking up with laughter as they took turns trying to maneuver their golf balls past a swinging, suspended log. To nearly all the kids, it seemed, the day was a blast—but not for Jackie. She could only think about her midnight fix. Cutting had become an escape she now turned to many times every day. And with a succession of disturbing dreams, she felt a greater urgency to seek its relief.

She found plenty of ways to do it secretly. Only a moment was needed to sneak away, reach into her pocket, and dig out her piece of glass or blade. She found privacy in the bathroom or the cubby hall. Chores offered more easy opportunities. She'd offer to take the sacks of garbage to the trash area or retrieve canned items from the food shed.

> Cutting had become an escape she now turned to many times every day. And with a succession of disturbing dreams, she felt a greater urgency to seek its relief.

The day's activities at the park dragged on, finally coming to an end. As Jackie and the others piled into the van to return to the Ranch, she huddled toward a window. The dream seemed to fill the glass next to her like a movie clip looping over and over. She closed her eyes, and it played across her eyelids. *So real. Stop. Go away.* At that moment, she couldn't deal with it. She couldn't cut, sleep, or escape.

The van pulled in at the Ranch and parked by the school building. She barely paid attention to the others around her, talking to each other, talking to her.

"Hey, Jackie, grab those water bottles."

She picked up the bottles.

Someone held up a sweatshirt. "Is this yours, Jackie?"

"No."

"Are you going up to the dorm before dinner, Jackie? Could you bring down my journal?"

"Yeah." *Whatever.* She couldn't share the invading thoughts. They wouldn't understand.

Step by slow step, she climbed the rock-lined stairs to her room. No one followed. Once inside, she sat on her bed and retrieved the hidden razor from her dresser. She stood and walked to the row of sinks and looked at the weary expression in the mirror. Leaning against a wall, she slid to the floor in one corner. Over and over, she cut her stomach and one arm.

> Not sure what to do next, Jackie stopped at the back door of the lodge kitchen. *I'm not going in there. Everyone will freak.*

As the relief started to wear away, fear began to set in. Jackie realized the cuts on her arm went deep. Still no one had come into the dorm area. The bleeding was too much for her to

SCARS THAT WOUND : SCARS THAT HEAL

take care of on her own. She pulled a sweater out of her drawer and tugged it on, then grabbed tissues to cover the arm wounds. She walked down the cement stairs, watching for someone she could tell.

Not sure what to do next, Jackie stopped at the back door of the lodge kitchen. *I'm not going in there. Everyone will freak.* She saw one of the interns, a young college student, pass through the hall and into the kitchen. Jackie caught her attention. She waved her toward the outside back deck.

The door swung open, then banged shut. Jackie held her hand tight over her injured arm. The bleeding hadn't stopped. She watched the intern's expression change from curiosity to worry.

"What happened, Jackie? Are you OK?"

Jackie's concern for her injury shifted to panic. She began to shake. Fear ran its icy fingers through her mind. *Something is after me.* Her eyes widened. She turned and ran around the corner of the deck to a ledge overlooking the trash area. Her stare locked on the hillside of oaks. *A shadow in the trees.* She crouched and pushed her body as close to the lodge wall as she could. "Something's in the trees," she mumbled. "It's going to get me."

Some of the other interns had come out to the deck as they realized something was happening with Jackie. One sat down next to her. Someone wiped and tended to her wounds. Another knelt in front of her. "What's wrong, Jackie? What happened?"

So afraid. So tired.

"What do you need? What can we do?"

Their voices seemed far away.

eight

"Do you want us to talk to John? We can call him."

"Jackie, is that what you want?"

She couldn't move. The fear was too much. She pushed herself against the building even more.

"I'll call John," one said.

Someone left. The others remained by Jackie and waited. She didn't want them to leave. Fear still pricked her skin. She shivered.

Soon she heard footsteps, then a man's voice, gentle and caring. Then quiet. He spoke again. She couldn't find her own voice, but she began to hear his words.

"Jackie, why don't we go downstairs? We can talk in my office." She tensed, then relaxed. John. She could let him help her walk. He would protect her.

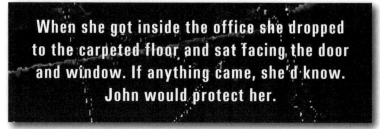

When she got inside the office she dropped to the carpeted floor and sat facing the door and window. If anything came, she'd know. John would protect her.

John lifted Jackie to her feet. His arms steadied her as they walked down an outdoor flight of stairs to his office. She clutched his arms, walked quickly. *Got to get to his office. Safe. I want to be safe.*

When she got inside the office she dropped to the carpeted floor and sat facing the door and window. If anything came, she'd know. John would protect her.

Many dreams and memories invaded Jackie's sleep over the next several months. As much as she could with John, Jackie talked through her feelings about the rape, and her newly stirred memories of the molestations from her past. As Christmas break approached, her anxiety reached new levels of intrusion. She wanted to go home for the holidays and see Mom and Dad and Nikki, but going there felt frightening. It meant getting near places and people that brought memories. She wasn't sure she could do it.

> Do not fear, for I am with you; do not anxiously look about you, for I am your God. I will strengthen you, surely I will help you, surely I will uphold you with My righteous right hand.
>
> ISAIAH 41:10

MEMORIES STIRRED

More and more often, as the memories of being molested invaded Jackie's thoughts and dreams, they stepped from a shadowy role into real life—*they had happened*. Remembering was painful, and escaping her thoughts and emotions grew nearly impossible.

Except through cutting.

To try to understand and face the memories of the molestations, Jackie wrote in her journals, talked to her counselor, and read books. One book described common symptoms of victims of abuse. "I could relate to every one," she said later. Her struggles and choices began to make sense.

She realized more connections between her childhood molestations and her self-abuse through cutting, burning, substance abuse, and sex.

At the Ranch, Jackie was only beginning to put words to her memories and emotions. Many of her initial counseling sessions with John were spent in silence or talking about safe subjects—like what happened that week at the work program. John said later, "There wasn't any real ability on her part to talk about the things that were bothering her. She had no words to express her feelings or what had happened to her."

She would talk when she was ready. John would wait.

Journaling proved to be a good outlet for Jackie. John agreed it was helpful for her: "It helps to put things into words. It's a way for somebody to begin to get around to actually telling something. Writing gets things out of your head and puts them outside of yourself for a while." John never required Jackie to keep or share any of her writing, but she often chose to use her journals in their sessions to explain what she had been thinking. She also wrote many letters to John, which helped her share her struggles honestly.

John saw Jackie's self-injury as her way of doing whatever it took to calm down. He helped her understand how her anxiety also was manifesting itself as a medical condition and how she could begin to manage it. The continued trauma of growing up with issues way beyond a child's ability to handle left Jackie especially sensitive. John began to see how her anxiety rose to a level where she imagined things like people hiding in the trees—as she did the day her dream overwhelmed her. "She probably didn't have any other thought except that it must be spiritual, and if it was, then it must be some kind of evil presence," he said. "I think for a while that was all she could chalk it up to."

John helped Jackie challenge her thinking. "We started working a lot on renewing the mind and helping her not to rely on her feelings as much as on what she knew to be true, especially about spiritual things." Around that time, Jackie wrote in her journal: *The way I view God I know is twisted, but I think that's changing slowly.*

Eventually Jackie began to think about talking more openly with her family about what she had gone through. She considered confronting some of her molesters. The promise of getting closer to the point of resolving the pain seemed hopeful, but thinking about even the first steps sent her to the steep edge of her emotions. She backed away in fear. In her journal she wrote: *I get glimpses of these people every now and then. I just go numb.* She continued to meet with John and talk through the options, but she didn't feel ready. More from her journal: *Being in a place of strength I'm not. I haven't given up responsibility. I still feel like I'm the one who should be punished. I couldn't possibly give over all the responsibility. That would be too easy.*

Jackie still carried the burden of the abuse that others—mostly adults—had forced onto her young mind and body. She so desperately hoped for freedom from that past.

> Someone who self-injures may be experiencing too many emotions and memories to handle at one time. If needed, be a resource person and help him find ministries or professionals that can bring greater insight into dealing with those thoughts and feelings.

So Many Stories

The threads of trauma within the stories of those who self-injure can be similar. Events and reasons look familiar. But in so many more ways, the stories are unique.

Not everyone comes up against deeply buried memories like Jackie did. You may have experienced abuse, as she did, and remember it all too clearly. Or you may have a painful history behind your choice to hurt yourself, and it has little or no connection to abuse. A few big events that turned your world upside down. Or a series of smaller ones over many years, stitching themselves into the fabric of who you are today. There is one certain commonality—some emotions, memories, or thoughts crucially important to you have added up to the feeling that self-injury is the way to manage the emotional fallout.

Memories sharpen into reality. Secrets are revealed. Understanding dawns. The past sits starkly before you. It threatens to pull you under. It sends you to the edge of impossible. It hurts deeply.

And it matters that it hurts.

As Christian Hill, a counselor, met with more and more teens who self-injure, he discovered that the self-abuse really isn't the problem. "It's the difficult thoughts, emotions, and behavior behind it," he says. One seventeen-year-old he met with told him she wanted to be "small and invisible so no one would notice her." She also told him, "Sometimes I get so anxious I don't feel comfortable in my own skin. Cutting helps release all this tension."

SCARS THAT WOUND : SCARS THAT HEAL

Others who self-injure shared about their emotional fallout:

"I grew up really angry and depressed."

"I felt like I had done everything wrong."

"I felt angry about the family God put me in."

"I felt that everything that ever happened to me was my fault."

"I was afraid my father would hurt me again."

"I felt alone when my mom attempted suicide and I was sent to live with a relative."

"I felt worthless and that I deserved to be punished."

"I was adopted; I felt rejected and abandoned."

"I didn't feel loved."

"I couldn't like myself."

And the list could grow with each unique set of circumstances and emotions—yours included.

But Kyle found there is always hope. "It's with my new relationship with God that I've come to realize that no matter what happens or who comes or goes from my life, I am *never* completely alone," he said.

Dan found comfort knowing he's not alone with his emotions. He said, "Jesus is a wounded healer. He can relate to damaged emotions, given the abuse and neglect he went through. He knows exactly what it feels like—I believe it helps him understand me even better."

Dan's right about Jesus.

The person who continues to self-injure isn't trying to make life miserable for you. Be a good model for her as you respond to any frustration you feel. Patiently talk through your observations, thoughts, and feelings. Show how to react calmly to difficult situations. Demonstrate how you trust God.

HOPE OF RENEWAL

If there is anyone who is willing to hear you out, it's Jesus. When you're mad, scared, anxious, or heartbroken, he's ready to listen. You can be entirely real and honest with him. He understands scars and wounds.

And he understands more.

Beaten and tortured, Jesus was led to the hill where soldiers nailed him to a cross and he died. But God had no intention that his Son's life would end there. Out of the darkness of betrayal and pain, Jesus rose again to life.

Life.

Jesus knows we need that kind of hope—out of the depths of pain that feels like death, life can come. Renewal is possible.

One of God's servants, King David, wrote, "Create in me a clean heart, O God, and renew a steadfast spirit within me" (Psalm 51:10). The prophet Isaiah wrote, "Those who hope in the Lord will renew their strength. They will soar on wings like eagles; they will run and not grow weary, they will walk and not be faint" (Isaiah 40:31, *NIV*). And Paul, one of the chief apostles in the New Testament, wrote, "Do not be conformed to this world, but be transformed by the renewing of your mind" (Romans 12:2).

Renewal means the promise of a new start. Like David, you can pray for a clean heart and restored courage to live the next day stronger than you were in the one before. God will give you a new beginning and a sense of freedom from your past.

Renewal means new strength. Trust God when you feel weak and weary. Trust him when you can't handle one more thought, emotion, betrayal, or hurt. Trust him when you feel the pull to turn to your tool of self-injury. He will give you what you need to push through the hardest moment and not give up.

Renewal means a new way of thinking. Conforming to the world is doing what you usually do, or what others do—the same routine, the same response. Instead, you can ask God to help you begin to think differently. He will help you learn to respond in better ways to the emotions and difficulties you face.

Renewal *is* possible. Jesus made sure of that. Get to know him better. You can honor who he is as God and still be entirely real with him—especially when you feel slammed with the emotions and pain of your past or your present.

Go talk to Jesus. Unsure how? Have a friend pray with you.

Go to Jesus with your emotions, your pain. He'll listen.

God, facing the pain in my life is tough, and sometimes I can't imagine getting through it without turning to the comfort and release of self-injury. It's even hard to admit that you have a better way for me to deal with everything. It's hard to trust that it could work. Thank you that I can be totally honest with you about this and about all my feelings and thoughts. Help me begin to do those things that will bring me into the full healing you have for me. Help me not to give up hope that you are listening and with me every step of the way. AMEN.

Everything that was created received its life from him, and his life gave light to everyone.

JOHN 1:3, 4 (CEV)

GOING DEEPER

■ The same responses to hurts and difficulties will keep you right where you are. What are some ways you can begin to "renew your mind" (Romans 12:2) by thinking differently and more hopefully about your life?

■ King David was courageous as he prayed for a new beginning in his life. What can courage look like in your life? Be specific—think and dream big.

■ Taking a look at your toughest struggles with self-injury, where do you need new strength to push through and not give up? What does trusting God in your life and through your struggles mean to you?

DEEPER STILL

Begin a journal if you haven't already. If you have, consider starting a new section, or a new kind of journal—one in which you write out not only your feelings and thoughts but also the encouragements that you've received from God to keep going.

nine

I'm starting to get way overwhelmed. I don't know what to do.
I'm scared of the unknown. I'm afraid of letting my mind
remember and of letting myself feel anything.

—Jackie's Journal

What day was it? Jackie traced the events of the last few days and remembered it was Tuesday. She tucked the crisp sheet around her and looked around the windowless room with its two beds—one empty, one occupied by her. The stark room had a desk and access to a bathroom and shower. The walls were white. Horribly, boring white.

Not surprising for a mental hospital.

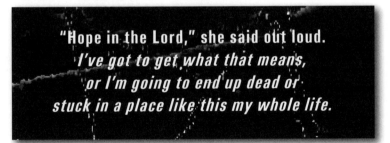

"Hope in the Lord," she said out loud. I've got to get what that means, or I'm going to end up dead or stuck in a place like this my whole life.

A song had been running through her mind—a praise song she heard once while riding in one of the Ranch vehicles. Its lyrics were from Psalm 131: "I (do not) involve myself in great matters, or in things too difficult for me. Surely I have composed and quieted my soul . . . hope in the Lord."

She used the stub of a pencil issued by the hospital staff to write the words on scraps of paper. She had written them over and over during the two days she had been here. "Hope in the Lord," she said out loud. *I've got to get what that means, or I'm going to end up dead or stuck in a place like this my whole life.*

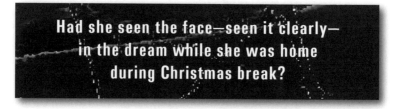

Had she seen the face—seen it clearly—in the dream while she was home during Christmas break?

She had arrived here early on Sunday morning after a night of terror. Late Saturday, all her whirling thoughts had converged into a storm of fear and anxiety. She felt as if she were being blown over an emotional cliff. She had wanted to talk to her family about it, help them understand, but she didn't. The insistent dreams continued to invade her sleep. Had she seen the face—seen it clearly—in the dream while she was home during Christmas break? Even if she had, she was afraid to accuse. Afraid she was wrong. Splicing memories together created a picture that made sense, but she wasn't sure. Opportunities to talk to her family came and went—both during and after Christmas break. John offered to help, but she couldn't bring herself to do it. And if she never could have that conversation, would she ever get well?

In her room at the dorm, the months of doubts and questioning spiraled into hopelessness and depression. At times, the thought of suicide entered her mind. Then one night the depth and location of each cut became more deliberate. Her purpose moved beyond temporary relief. The possibility that she could really go through with ending her life scared her, and she sought help. "I know I'm not safe," she told Debbie, one of the Ranch staff. The night of fear blurred into talks with the counselors. Finally she agreed—John and Debbie should take her to the local hospital.

Once there, she faced an ER doctor who didn't believe she was doing anything more than her usual cutting. Though weary, she was determined to convince him. It was definitely more. She was sure of it.

"We've gone over this," the doctor told her. "You're cutting yourself like you have in the past."

"No. This is different. I don't want to live anymore."

He sighed and jotted down a few notes. "Fine. I'll see where there's an opening."

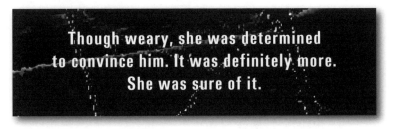

Though weary, she was determined to convince him. It was definitely more. She was sure of it.

At least he was going to do something. She didn't want to go to a mental hospital, but she didn't know where the anxiety she felt might lead. She needed protection and safety.

It was early morning when a sheriff's deputy arrived to take her to a Sacramento treatment center. Jackie was escorted outside. "Do I have to wear the handcuffs?" she asked the officer.

nine

He opened the cruiser's back door. "Nope. You'll be fine back here," he answered.

Jackie climbed into the cramped backseat behind a cage barrier. The door slammed closed. She heard a knock on the cruiser's door. It was John. He handed her backpack to the officer.

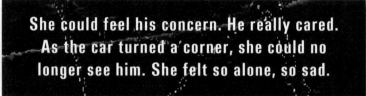

She could feel his concern. He really cared. As the car turned a corner, she could no longer see him. She felt so alone, so sad.

The car pulled away from the curb, and Jackie kept her eyes on John. He had helped her through those awful hours at the Ranch and then waited through her time in the ER. She could feel his concern. He really cared. As the car turned a corner, she could no longer see him. She felt so alone, so sad.

The first two days at the treatment center were a blur. She slept a lot, wrote with her pencil stub, and had a few short visits from others that broke the monotony. Her parents came on Sunday. They looked sad.

"I'm so sorry," Jackie kept saying. She didn't want to put them through any more than she had already.

Nikki didn't come. Why not? Was she mad? Jackie wiped her eyes.

On that Tuesday afternoon, the hospital staff gave Jackie her clothes and transferred her to another room. She had a

SCARS THAT WOUND : SCARS THAT HEAL

roommate in this one, and a window with a view of a courtyard. John visited; that made her day. "I think I'm ready to talk to my parents," she told him.

Debbie visited on Wednesday. She brought a poem for Jackie that wished her peace and hope. Jackie picked up the poem from the side table and reread it.

Hope-Painted Glasses

Despair overwhelming
destruction threatening
If only you could see . . .
Peace in dream-filled slumber,
quieted thoughts during wakeful leisure
integrity in bonds—storge, phileo, eros
the seasoning of agape
acceptance of the whole
a good work complete
desires fulfilled.
Pain is but for a night
Joy comes in the morning.[1]

Hold on for the blessings. They do come.
I love you, Jackie.

Debbie

Tears stung her eyes as she looked up from the page to scan the stark hospital room. She longed to be well. *I'm holding on, Lord. I'm trying to hope.*

In the middle of that night she heard screaming from a man down the hall. She couldn't see around a wall to the open

---

1. Debbie Isom, author; personal poem shared with the author; October 2, 2006.

door, but she heard objects crashing and banging and the sharp, crackling sound of Tasers as police subdued the man.

Afraid and confused, she curled up in her bed and begged her body to settle down and sleep. As the night quieted, her mind and heart still raced. Eventually they slowed, and she relaxed and fell asleep.

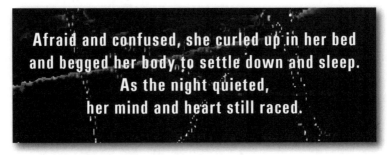

Afraid and confused, she curled up in her bed and begged her body to settle down and sleep. As the night quieted, her mind and heart still raced.

She dreamed that her sister, Nikki, came to visit her at the hospital. Nikki sat in the corner of Jackie's room, looking peaceful, and then began to sing for Jackie. It was the Christmas song "O Come, O Come, Emmanuel."

O Come, O Come, Emmanuel, and ransom captive Israel.

In her dream, Jackie concentrated on the words and her sister's sweet voice.

That mourns in lonely exile here, until the Son of God appear.

Jackie closed her eyes and dropped into a deep rest; this was all still part of her dream. The peace she felt eased itself into her real-world sleep.

> Let the morning bring me word of your unfailing love,
> for I have put my trust in you.
> Show me the way I should go,
> for to you I lift up my soul.
>
> PSALM 143:8 (NIV)

WEIGHING THE CHOICES

Jackie wanted to face her past and confront those involved, including her family's way of dealing with her pain and their responses to her. She saw the possibilities of a more peaceful and productive life, one that didn't involve self-injury to cope. But she also wrestled greatly with all of this. There were many people and circumstances in her story over which she had no control. Would others listen? Would they care? Did they ever before? What would they say or do?

She didn't want to upset her family or burden them anymore. There were times when bringing up the past felt like betrayal. Was there a sacrifice involved? If there was, would it be hers to make?

The memories, the clash of thoughts, the what-ifs, the responsibility for others—the pieces wouldn't come together. Change seemed crazily out of reach and options carried huge risk. She wrote in her journal that she was afraid that any day John might say, "*I don't know how to help you anymore. I don't know what to do with you. You're on your own.*" Her next written words were: *I don't know which is scarier—John saying that or me having to live without my cutting. This is all too much for my brain.*

I have something to cut with, so I'll be all right. I have a whole lot of anxiety, which feels like anger. But if I can smile and sleep, I can make it through one more day.

Then the day arrived when making it through one more twenty-four-hour period didn't seem possible. The cuts went dangerously deeper. Thankfully, she immediately got help.

Debbie had been meeting with Jackie regularly for Bible study and to give her encouragement. She was one of those Jackie turned to for help the night her self-injury felt dangerously out of control. Debbie talked with Jackie that night about ways she could make herself safe and stay at the Ranch, but Jackie didn't feel that would be enough. She couldn't get through the night. "She had spent a lot of time developing relationships at the Ranch and that had become her safety net," Debbie recalled. "That night her safety net wasn't big enough. If she stayed, she risked putting herself beyond what we could offer her."

After her five-day hospital stay, Jackie returned to the Ranch. She wasn't going to give up. John saw that quality in her. "She's a fighter, and she's had such a hard life to fight against," he said. John had encouraged her to see that trait in her life. He would always tell her, "You're just not a giver-upper." And he saw that again when she returned from the hospital. "She came out of there with a different perspective: 'If my only option is going to the hospital, I don't ever want to do that again. I want to do something else.'"

That new perspective would involve taking chances that could be tough. John recognized that for Jackie it meant "realizing that if she was going to get better, she was going to have to open up and start to do some things that she wasn't doing. Take some chances, like talking to her parents or just talking in general about what was going on, and letting it out."

Jackie did begin to talk more. She talked to her mom, her dad, and Nikki. There was some listening, and there were reactions of being deeply saddened by what they heard. But in the end, she didn't feel anyone really got it. John still saw the benefit in her taking this step. "It was actually helpful for her to get to the point where she realized, 'OK, I can't rely on my family because they're not going to do this for me.' That was hard for Jackie—but also realistic. So it was, 'OK, if that's not going to work, then I'm going to have to do something else.'"

Jackie could move toward being OK, even if others didn't move as she hoped they would.

The next several months at the Ranch were filled with both progress and struggles. Jackie set up her own accountability. Said Debbie of that step, "She tried not to leave loopholes so she could cut. If she felt the impulse to cut, she got to where she could express that before she did it. And if she did cut, she told us." Debbie realized that though Jackie was striving for accountability, she still maintained her "secret spots." Debbie added, "Sometimes people just shift their self-injury to some place where no one will see it, or they shift *how* they do it. Jackie's degree of healing went only as far as she was able to be open and honest about what she was doing."

Jackie's efforts were evident. She felt the continued support of the staff, her friends at the Ranch, and her family, to the extent that they were able to give it. Jackie completed the program. She knew setbacks might come, but she was determined to not give up.

Setbacks can be scary and frustrating for the person who self-injures—and for you as their friend and support person. To understand their struggle, put it in the context of something you wrestle with. Overcoming isn't easy or automatic. Continue to care for and be patient with your friend.

NEVER ALONE

A big part of Jackie's ability to speak out more and to honestly face how she was going to get better was her growing confidence that God was with her. But what does it mean that God is *with* you?

It meant a lot for the Israelites, who were leaving their desert life to go live in the lush land God had planned for them. But before—and while—they traveled through the desert, God had shown his presence and provision through many miracles. Now they stood in sight of the vast, rich land where they could rest from their desert travels. But they also knew that in order to move into it they would face many battles, and they were afraid. God assured their leader, Joshua, that he and the people would succeed no matter what they went through. God said, "Have I not commanded you? Be strong and courageous! Do not tremble or be dismayed, for the Lord your God is with you wherever you go" (Joshua 1:9). God was fully aware of what the Israelites were about to face, and he urged them to go forward out of the desert, through the battles, and into the place of rest he had prepared for them.

Moving toward healing isn't easy. You probably have already faced many battles. With the strong possibility that more are ahead, the desert may seem like a pretty comfortable place to set up your tent. But before you pound in the stakes, ask God to help you see what your life would look like with the fullness and rest he has prepared for you. As you take more steps toward that life, know he is with you through every painful or difficult moment. And if you need to stop and rest to remember and believe again, he won't mind. He'll stay with you. His plans are for you to succeed.

God, it's hard to take chances and believe that something different and good can be ahead for me. Help me believe. Give me not only a clear picture of the richness of what you have in mind for me, but also a clear understanding of what I've been settling for. Help me want your best for me. Give me the strength and courage to go forward toward it. And when it gets hard, remind me you are with me and will help me succeed. AMEN.

The Lord will give strength to His people;
The Lord will bless His people with peace.

PSALM 29:11

GOING DEEPER

■ God is aware of all you've experienced and any battles you might face as you go forward in your healing. What fears and concerns remain for you in what lies ahead?

■ God is *with* you. What does—or can—that look like in your life? In particular, in your healing from self-injury?

■ Joshua didn't go into battle alone. And Jackie had John, Debbie, and others alongside her as she fought, weak as she was at times. Who do you have alongside you to provide support and encourage you when you experience setbacks?

DEEPER STILL

Spread out the largest piece of paper you can find. Draw pictures or write your thoughts describing what a full and restful life would hold for you. When you're done, write a statement of success. An example: "I will overcome this because God is with me."

ten

You have shown me the meaning of "the love of Christ."
You have shown me that I'm worth something more
than I could have ever imagined.

—Jackie's Journal

"Come on up, Jackie," John said.

Every Sunday, the students, interns, and staff transformed the lodge living room into a church. This was Jackie's last Sunday as a Ranch student. Today she would move into town to live in the "Girls' House"—a transition home for the young women who had finished the program. Traditionally, the Ranch "prayed in" every person who came and, when each completed their stay, they were "prayed out."

> John placed his hand on her shoulder. "It's a good day to celebrate what you've begun here at the Ranch and what God has been doing in your life."

Jackie went to the front and stood next to John while he read the names of those who would pray for her. Soon twelve others surrounded Jackie, including Sue, Debbie, and John. Jackie's smile carved into her deep dimples.

John placed his hand on her shoulder. "It's a good day to celebrate what you've begun here at the Ranch and what God has been doing in your life."

Jackie shot a quick glance toward her parents and Tom and Melody, who were watching. She felt their support in their big smiles.

> Her stomach fluttered with excitement and nervousness. Over the next few weeks, she'd sign up for classes and start looking for a job. She wanted to do well.

John lifted his hand off Jackie's shoulder and thumbed through a book in his hand. "I want to read a quote out of Hannah Hurnard's book, *Hinds' Feet on High Places*—a story that's been an encouragement to you these past months. Let's see." He adjusted his glasses, then summarized a portion of the story. "This is where the crippled character, Much Afraid, is given new feet and a new name, Grace and Glory. The Shepherd tells her, 'Now you are able to run, leaping on the mountains and able to follow me wherever I go, so that we need never be parted again.'[1] That's how Jesus sees you, Jackie. He's given you what you need to always follow him." John looked toward the others surrounding Jackie. "Let's pray."

Later that day, Jackie moved into the Girls' House—a large, white, 1940s-era home in an old neighborhood. Her stomach

---

1. Hannah Hurnard, *Hinds' Feet on High Places* (Carol Stream, Illinois: Tyndale, 1975), 242.

fluttered with excitement and nervousness. Over the next few weeks, she'd sign up for classes and start looking for a job. She wanted to do well.

Jackie stood in front of the local Christian bookstore and caught a glimpse of her reflection in the door. She ran her fingers through her long, dark hair and made sure it fell over the front of her shoulders. Her baby blue tank top with its matching sweater covered the scars on her arms. *Good.* She looked casual but nice in her tan skirt and flip-flops. She had to get this job. She pushed open the door and heard the tinkling of the bells that hung from the doorframe.

She scanned the store and spotted a woman behind the counter. This was probably Amy, one of the workers in the family-owned business. Amy would be doing the interview. She looked like she was probably in her fifties. She had cropped, blond hair and, as she turned toward Jackie, flashed a pleasant smile.

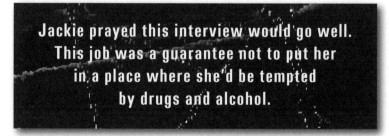

Jackie prayed this interview would go well. This job was a guarantee not to put her in a place where she'd be tempted by drugs and alcohol.

Jackie greeted her and returned a smile. "Hi. I'm here to interview for a job."

"Jaclyn? Come on in." Amy stepped from behind the counter, shook Jackie's hand, then turned and walked toward the back of the store. "We'll go back here where we can have some privacy."

They entered a small room, where some of the store's products were stored. Amy invited Jackie to have a seat next to a desk. Jackie prayed this interview would go well. This job was a guarantee not to put her in a place where she'd be tempted by drugs and alcohol.

Jackie stilled her shaking legs as Amy's friendliness eased her into sharing a little about her life and her time at the Ranch. She didn't tell Amy about her cutting, but she admitted her past struggle with drugs. She still wasn't over the cutting, and she was glad the signs of it were safely hidden from view.

The interview went quickly and seemed to go well. Amy asked a few final questions and then wrapped it up. "Jaclyn, thank you for coming in. I'll call you next week and let you know our decision."

Jackie smiled. She still felt the nervousness through her entire body, but she managed a "Thanks."

As she walked through the store she hoped more than anything she'd get the job. She had visited this place many times to make purchases. The employees were always nice and the atmosphere was peaceful. She opened the door to leave and again heard the tinkling of those bells. Her one thought as she left was her hope that she'd hear that sound many more times.

Jackie entered the bookstore to the familiar sound of the bells. She smiled. She'd been working at the store for several months now and enjoyed it as much as she thought she would. She felt the midsummer sun warming the store as she let the door close. She headed toward the back room and dropped off her lunch.

She turned to help Amy open the store, then stopped. She had forgotten her sweater. To that day, no one in the store had seen the scars on her arms. As she moved around the aisles of books and gifts, vacuuming and then straightening items on the shelves, she kept her body turned from Amy. Then it was time to count the money and get the register ready. At any moment the "Open" sign would be flipped and customers would begin to enter. How would she hide her arms then? She was growing more nauseous by the moment.

She turned to help Amy open the store, then stopped. She had forgotten her sweater.

She crossed her arms and went to Amy. "I forgot my sweater. Can I run home real quick and get it?"

She watched Amy's puzzled glance move from her face to her arms and back to her face.

"Sure, go ahead."

Jackie let out a sigh of relief. She was comfortable wearing short sleeves around the Ranch and now in front of her new roommates, but revealing her arms at this job was a different story.

A few days later she was working at the register. Amy placed a stack of books on the counter and turned to her. "Do you remember the other day when you went to get your sweater? I have to tell you that I noticed a lot of scars on your arms."

"I remember." *Where is this going?*

"I didn't have a clue what to think. I asked my brother, Richard, about what I saw. I thought he might know." With one hand, Amy shifted the books on the counter. "He struggled as a teen and into his adult life. He told me he had seen a lot of young women who cut themselves. When I asked him why, he said that it has something to do with a release of deep pain. Sometimes it's because of drugs or difficult emotions. In these girls' minds, to cut themselves feels good." Amy looked at Jackie's covered arms. "Do you want to tell me what this is for you?"

Jackie felt Amy's concern. "I do cut, but it's not drug-related," she said as tears began to pool in her eyes.

"I don't understand how hurting yourself like that can feel good, but I will believe that in your world of pain, it does." Amy paused and watched Jackie for a moment before going on. "This has to be something you do in secret."

"Yeah, it is."

"You know, you don't have to cover up your arms here. You don't have to be ashamed. Where you are now with Christ, those scars can become a testimony rather than a secret. Maybe to talk about it can free you from the secret. Use your story to praise God and show others that he heals not only physically, but emotionally and spiritually."

Jackie nodded as tears streamed freely down her cheeks. She had been afraid of how people who didn't know her well would react to the many scars on her arms. Amy didn't judge her. Maybe others wouldn't either.

> And we, who with unveiled faces all reflect the Lord's glory, are being transformed into his likeness with ever-increasing glory, which comes from the Lord, who is the Spirit.
>
> 2 Corinthians 3:18 (NIV)

NO MORE SWEATER

Jackie left the Ranch with a new perspective of her relationship with God and a plan to stay in healthy relationships with others. "The Ranch was my support, and I really tried to keep in contact," she recalled. "I continued to surround myself with good people that I trusted. I was really scared I would get in with the wrong crowd again."

As she applied for jobs, she avoided places where she'd heard there might be drugs. "The Christian bookstore was the one I really wanted," she said. "When you go into that store, it's very peaceful—you could stay there all day. I felt it would be a very good thing for me to be a part of."

Amy sensed that working at the store meant more than just a job to Jackie. "I saw a sweetness and a hope in her that touched my heart," she said. She remembered that first time she saw Jackie's scars. "When she had her arms crossed like she was cold, I saw multiple one-inch and one-and-a-half-inch scars. I wasn't repulsed, just confused—what had this young girl gone through?"

A few days later, after Amy spoke to her brother, she decided to talk to Jackie.

"I prayed about it. A beautiful young girl who hurts herself—I felt that I needed to say something, not to accuse her, not to condemn her. She wanted to cover her past with her sweater, but that only kept her in a dark, secret place filled with guilt and shame. In reality it gave her permission to keep doing what she was doing."

Over the months, Amy talked to Jackie often about Jesus' complete forgiveness of her. "When Jaclyn fully agreed with God, she was able to get rid of the sweater, bear her arms, and freely live in God's truth," Amy said. "Through Christ, God heals the soul, the spirit, and the emotions and makes us whole." She spoke of the freedom that Jackie discovered. "Jaclyn is free from the lie that she deserves to cut herself. She is free from the lie that this form of destruction feels good. She's free from the burden of guilt." Then Amy added, with a smile, "And she is free to wear some really cute clothes."

Jackie recalled—with a form of relief—the day Amy brought her scars into the open. "I was shocked that Amy said I didn't have to worry about hiding my scars. I didn't know what people's reactions were going to be. So it felt good." This was a powerful turning point for Jackie. She began to feel comfortable wearing short sleeves and letting others, even strangers, see her scars.

A few days after Jackie's talk with Amy, she went into work excited that she had shared this story with the residents at the Ranch. "I showed the scars on my arms and told them God was healing me," she said.

At that time, Jackie still cut a couple times a week—when she felt especially anxious. She'd cut on her legs so the wounds would be hidden. Amy fully believed that God planned for Jackie to work at the bookstore and be encouraged through more people who knew and loved him. "She was covering up," Amy said. "That's the part God had me deal with."

Amy and the owners of the store—Jay, Stephanie, and Judy—became like family to Jackie. They surrounded her with love and support. God would use them to help Jackie through another important step in her journey to heal from self-injury.

> Talking about self-injury with someone who does it brings the choice out into the open and makes it something that's OK to talk about. But as you do, keep your thoughts in check. Stay compassionate and nonjudgmental.

Choices That Make a Difference

Jackie discovered that some situations were easier to avoid if she identified them and made a plan. She knew which social situations would be hard for her. She chose to live in a community and a house where she had strong support, and she chose which friends would be best to help her continue to make good choices. She held out for a job she knew had a positive environment, one without temptations that would take her back toward drugs or alcohol.

Making choices doesn't mean giving up everything you like. Ericka loved music too much to give it up. For her it came down to deciding which songs were best for her to listen to, and she took a bunch of songs off her iPod. "Music is just one part of my life that won't go away, but I can be a better girl and not listen to songs like 'Strawberry Gashes,'" Ericka says. "That's just asking for trouble."

Ryan cut mostly when he got angry. "Fights with my mother particularly triggered me," he said. "Always being a quiet person, cutting was my outlet." He now chooses to talk to others instead of cutting.

Dwelling on her past is one of Alisa's triggers, so her choices involved her thoughts. "I chose not to stay in the past," she said. "I chose to be a child of God, fully loved and forgiven. If I have feelings like I'm going to self-injure, I try not to be alone."

Jena tries to stay away from people and situations that bring out the urge for her to cut. It's still hard at times, but when the thoughts come back, she said, they're also a good sign she's not staying close to God. "Making the choice to get in touch with God again and to get some help from somebody is the best thing I can do for myself. Life doesn't get easier, but God gives us peace. He promises."

Some situations remain impossible to avoid. Suddenly the urges or triggers are right in front of you, with hardly a warning. Here's what Ericka, Jena, Dan, and others do.

> "I call someone up and talk about my thoughts and feelings."

> "I put on some good music and sing."

> "I go work out, like run or some other kind of exercise."

> "I pray and tell myself the truths about what God says about me: I'm God's friend. He loves me. He calls me beloved. He died for me. He cares about me."

"I put on my headphones and listen to soothing music so I drown out my negative thoughts."

"I get a friend and go do something to get my mind off things."

"I tell my mom I'm having a hard time and need her help to keep me safe."

"I cuddle or talk to my pets. Scrunch, my rabbit, is a great listener."

"I change activities: watch TV, read a book, or pray."

These kinds of activities will help you get past the initial minutes of wanting to hurt yourself. Instead, you choose to do something with the feelings or anxiety you feel—other than self-injure.

Susan Bowman, author of *See My Pain*, cautions that it can be difficult to buy into an alternative method until you find one that works. She says commitment "takes time and patience."

Susan Cook helps those she counsels generate a list of "supportive relationships and activities that encourage self-expression and create more positive feelings"—anything from writing poetry or creating collages to making time to care for yourself or putting a shelf in order. Another, she says, might be "listening to specific music that makes you feel better." She says one idea by itself may not feel like enough, but putting three or four together might. She also suggests developing a list of options that will lead to strong, healthy decisions when the impulse to self-injure is especially strong, or when it hits at two in the morning.

Both counselors see tremendous value in discovering and developing personal strengths. "Every individual has personal, God-given strengths that can help them through difficult times in their lives," Susan Bowman says.

Jackie developed a list of healthy options as well. "My counselor would suggest different things to control my anxiety—breathing, exercising, and counting. I had to be willing to try things people suggested no matter how stupid it sounded. I learned stuff like that really does work."

Mari and her counselor created a list of positive characteristics about herself. "I was to read this list every day," she said. She also has tried alternatives such as popping a rubber band on her wrist or rubbing ice cubes on her thighs. But, she said, "The goal is not to do anything to even want to self-injure."

Creative activities like working with clay, reflective journaling, drawing, painting, or playing an instrument are other ways to manage pain and emotions, redirect thoughts, and distract yourself from urges to self-injure.

For crisis situations, your plan might involve knowing who you're going to call. Susan Cook offers some practical questions to consider: "Are they programmed into your phone? Do you typically have access to your phone? If they are peers, are they allowed to answer the phone past 10 PM?"

> One way you can help a person who self-injures is to assist her in creating a support network. Ask her what activities she enjoys and help her find safe places and groups where she can enjoy those things.

Jackie and others decided they no longer wanted to give in to triggers and urges to self-injure. They chose to work toward ending their self-injury. It takes having a plan, tackling that plan one decision at a time, and keeping a firm "I'm not giving up" attitude even in the face of setbacks.

Have a plan: "I will" statements are powerful and purposeful. Three from the Psalms are: "My heart says of you, 'Seek his face!' Your face, Lord, I will seek" (Psalm 27:8, *NIV*); "When I am afraid, I will trust in you" (Psalm 56:3, *NIV*); and "I will meditate on all your works and consider all your mighty deeds" (Psalm 77:12, *NIV*). "I will" statements can be about trusting God as well as about specific actions. Make them realistic for you and build up to stronger commitments.

Take one decision at a time: Prayer is a natural companion to tackling each choice each day. God's design for you is freedom from anything that is self-harmful and discovery of what it is to rest fully in him. Invite him in on your "one decision at a time." John 14:14 says, "If you ask Me anything in My name, I will do it." As you ask God, you can trust that he has the very best in mind for you.

Think "I'm not giving up": Even when you face setbacks, you can choose to get back on course and refuse to quit. Don't let old habits imprison you. Have this attitude, found in Galatians 5:1: "It was for freedom that Christ set us free; therefore keep standing firm and do not be subject again to a yoke of slavery."

Christ set you free. Through your relationship and connection with him, over time you will be able to experience that freedom in a fuller sense. Before you know it, fewer and fewer situations will knock you off balance.

God, the relief that I get through hurting myself is only temporary freedom. It's not anything like the freedom you have in mind for me. What would my life be like without self-injury? What would it feel like to not carry the pain, hurts, and anxiety that I feel right now? God, help me begin to catch a glimpse of that kind of freedom. Give me strength to make purposeful choices to know you and trust you more. I want to keep moving toward the fullness of life you have in mind for me and not give up. AMEN.

> **Now the Lord is the Spirit,**
> **and where the Spirit of the Lord is, there is freedom.**
> 2 CORINTHIANS 3:17 (NIV)

GOING DEEPER

▪ Plans and goals set in motion offer hope. They start with your thoughts. Looking at some of the Psalms listed in this chapter, what are some ways you can move your thoughts in a healing and hopeful direction?

▪ Asking God for what is good for you and will promote your healing will help you begin to live in freedom. What good things for your healing do you want to ask him for right now?

▪ Part of good planning involves taking into consideration the possibility of setbacks. How might you be better prepared to tackle old habits and desires?

DEEPER STILL

Ask God to help you write a few "I will" statements that are uniquely yours. Start with a few simple ones and, as you're able to accomplish those, add more.

eleven

I found out that Nikki became a Christian, and she was totally stoked about God and being saved. It was so cool. I'm so happy.

—Jackie's Journal

"HEY, JACKIE!" Nikki was calling to her sister from the other side of the Ranch living room. "Sit next to me."

Jackie smiled at her sister and waded through the people standing and chatting. The Sunday morning worship was about to begin.

The two hugged and settled into folding chairs in the front row. Christmas was a couple weeks away. The lights strung around the walls and the decorated tree in the corner made the room feel warm and festive. Jackie noticed a wreath of five candles sitting on a small, cloth-covered table near the podium up front.

Now Nikki was doing well at the Ranch, and Jackie felt they were growing closer as sisters and friends.

She met her sister's eyes and grinned. Four months before, Nikki had arrived at the Ranch to be a resident. At nineteen, she had been living at home with their parents and couldn't keep a job for longer than a month and a half. She had an unhealthy relationship with a boyfriend and struggled with depression and bulimia. But now Nikki was doing well at the Ranch, and Jackie felt they were growing closer as sisters and friends. What Jackie really wanted right now was for the service to start. A few days before, Nikki had told her sister that she had a surprise for her.

Everyone settled into their chairs, and a small worship band opened the service with Christmas hymns. One was "O Come, O Come Emmanuel." Jackie hadn't heard that song since she dreamt of Nikki singing it to her while she was in the hospital. Jackie glanced toward Nikki, and her sister smiled. Was this the surprise? Jackie sang the song with everything in her.

> How present God had felt to her when she was in the hospital the last time. And since then he felt even more near and real as he led her to a great job and brought Nikki to the Ranch.

The song leaders stepped aside and Marvin, one of the staff members, stood and walked to the front. With his towering figure and direct manner, he talked passionately about the candle wreath. He called it an Advent wreath. While he lit two of its five candles, he shared how the wreath's symbolism was used to celebrate God's Son coming to the world as a baby. "Jesus is called Emmanuel," Marvin said. "This means 'God with us.'"

There it was again—Emmanuel. She smiled. How present God had felt to her when she was in the hospital the last time.

And since then he felt even more near and real as he led her to a great job and brought Nikki to the Ranch.

Marvin finished his talk by lighting one more candle. As he sat down, Nikki and one of the interns at the ranch, Amber, stood and turned to face everyone. They both had helped with worship before, so Jackie knew they were about to sing. With piano accompaniment, the two girls began the song "O Come, O Come Emmanuel."

This had to be the surprise. Tears quickly came to Jackie. As Nikki and Amber wove beautiful harmonies, Jackie felt overwhelmed with emotions. God had come to be a powerful part of their family. He had come to transform each of them. The joy that flooded in felt overwhelming. She hadn't felt this happy in a long time.

Jackie sat amazed as the rest of the service continued to emphasize Emmanuel—God with us. Even the sermon focused on that message. To Jackie, all of it was a solid message of God's encouragement and love.

After the sermon, sharing time started. Individuals began to share prayer requests and things they were thankful for. Jackie tried to gather the courage to tell everyone what the song and service had meant to her. Her legs shook, and she shifted in her chair. Should she tell them about the hospital dream? She hadn't told very many people. Huge tears began to fall down her cheeks, and she raised her hand.

"OK." She took a deep breath. "I have to share this. When I was in the hospital, I had a dream that Nikki came to visit me." Jackie related the events of the dream and wiped away more tears as she talked. Plenty of others were wiping at their own eyes by now.

eleven

"That dream and that song changed my perspective," Jackie told the group. "I felt an assurance that God was with me." Her voice broke and the tears began to flow freely. She quickly finished her story.

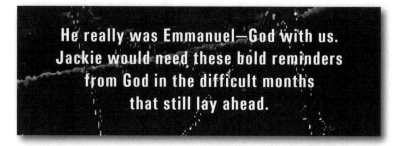

He really was Emmanuel—God with us. Jackie would need these bold reminders from God in the difficult months that still lay ahead.

When the service ended she hugged her sister, then turned to Amber. "You have no idea how huge it is for me that you sang that song or how many times I prayed for my sister to come to the Ranch."

Jackie draped her arm around Nikki's shoulders and squeezed her. The song recalled God's gift of hope while Jackie had been in the hospital. And now her sister was at the Ranch and learning to make better choices for her own life.

He really was Emmanuel—God with us.

Jackie would need these bold reminders from God in the difficult months that still lay ahead.

> "Behold, the virgin shall be with child and shall bear a son and they shall call his name Immanuel," which translated means, "God with us."
>
> MATTHEW 1:23

To Jackie, much had felt confusing, painful, and out of her control, yet she was learning that God was present and working in amazing ways in her life and in her family. Holding her family together wasn't a responsibility she needed to carry. Fixing what felt broken wasn't up to her. Even her own healing could be left in God's loving and capable hands. Jackie was able to accept these things more and more only as she understood how he really was *with* her.

That truth began to work in her mind and heart after she dreamt of her sister singing to her while she was in the hospital. Mike, the Ranch director, remembered that time as being one of Jackie's lowest as a Christian, but has no doubt that the song's message, from her dream, gave Jackie hope. "The dream itself chokes me up a little," Mike said. "I remember (Jackie) telling me about it. At that time Nikki was completely outside of Christ. She had made a childhood commitment but wasn't living her life for the Lord and wasn't a spiritual encouragement to Jackie."

Nikki remembered that "when my parents went to the hospital, I didn't go. I had a really cruddy and selfish attitude about Jackie being there, and I didn't want anything to do with it."

Jackie recalled, "I was really upset Nikki didn't come to visit me in the hospital, so to dream about her when I was really mad—it was just really neat how God used her in that. I finally told her about the dream."

eleven

Months later, Nikki went to the Ranch to tackle the problems of her own life. Not long before Christmas, she and Amber began to practice for a holiday service. As that Sunday drew nearer, Nikki hinted to Jackie that she had a surprise for her. For Jackie, just knowing her sister was staying at the Ranch—safe and doing well—already was giving her joy. "Nikki was growing, and our relationship was more open and honest. She was enjoying life again. Every time I'd go out to the Ranch, she was always laughing, and that was something I hadn't seen in a long time. She was learning a lot about herself and about God."

When Nikki and Amber began to sing that morning, Jackie became overwhelmed with joy. "Last time I heard that song," Jackie said, "I was in the hospital, and Nikki was out running around doing who knows what—both of us were so lost. Now we were both in a church service with our church family, experiencing God's love and experiencing it together. I was so overwhelmed with emotions."

Those who were involved in the service that day remembered they hadn't decided the focus would be "Emmanuel—God with us." Mike said, "It wasn't planned by anyone other than the Holy Spirit. 'God is with us' kept coming back over and over. What happened when Nikki sang was truly inspirational. God orchestrated that, and it involved both Jackie and Nikki."

Jackie kept praying for her family. "My hope for us was that we could all have an honest relationship with each other and that we would sincerely know the Lord as a family and grow in him," she said. "I wanted what I felt from the people here at the Ranch to overflow to my family. There are sincere people out there who really care about others. The love and care I had been experiencing, I wanted for them."

Even through the menacing shadows of the choices she had made, the family struggles, and the violations from the molestations she suffered, Jackie caught glimpses of hope. She longed to know forgiveness of others and forgiveness of herself. Would she? Would she ever get past the raw pain that still ripped through her heart?

> Forgiveness of others can be a big issue for the self-injurer. Be aware that forgiving doesn't immediately erase years of pain. Allow him to talk about the hurt while he's working through the forgiveness.

FORGIVENESS AS A PROCESS

Somewhere along the way, Jackie's anger and frustration toward her family began shifting to forgiveness and wanting good things for them. God's loving presence in Jackie's life had overflowed into how she viewed each member. She could still be hurt by some of their words and actions, and sometimes that made her sad or angry, but she kept praying for each one. She wanted them to experience growth to the same extent she had found it in her relationships—with God and with others.

Beginning to have that kind of hope for others involves forgiveness on some level, but getting over the hurt isn't as easy. Mari confronted her father, who abused her, and then felt deep frustration that he wouldn't apologize. She realized she hadn't forgiven him at first. Even when she did, healing from the pain of the past was still a difficult process. "I don't feel anger toward him any longer," Mari said. "It still hurts, but that is lessening." Mari wisely understood that forgiveness didn't mean she should allow her father to continue to hurt her. "I won't support his actions anymore or continue to lie about the past," she said.

Kyle has been working through feelings of rejection and abandonment from his family. He said, "While I will never be able to forget the pains of the past, I have been able to forgive and move on." Often he has needed to initiate the first steps, but in communicating and forgiving he hopes to "find closure and move on to a new beginning."

Forgiving doesn't mean that you have to deny the hurt you have experienced or that you feel now. Said Dan, "I think I've tried to rush forgiveness without dealing with the hurt." At the same time, he has grown to recognize that "we are all fallen people in need of a righteous God."

A friend of Jackie's who prayed with her about forgiveness helped her take a different look at the people who hurt her. She helped Jackie see that because they didn't know God, they were capable of doing horrible things. "When my friend told me that, I didn't care," Jackie said. "They still did stuff to me. As we talked and prayed about it more, it became easier for me to start working on the process of forgiveness. Her answer satisfied something in me. They don't know God. They don't have Jesus. They don't have the same morals. I don't know how to explain it, but that changed how I looked at them."

Author Susan Bowman says that "forgiveness does not condone what someone has done, such as sexual abuse, but it releases the hold that person has on you."

Jena is still trying to figure out forgiveness of others in her life. "It takes a lot of work. I'm still in the process of forgiving people for the things they did, but even in just trying to work on it, God sees my heart, respects that, and will help me."

Healing from hurts takes time. Forgiveness is a part of keeping that healing moving forward. Wishing good for others, as Jackie did, can follow. God is with you in this part of the journey too.

> If you're a family member of someone who has turned to self-harming behavior, consider if you need to ask her forgiveness for anything. Also, some who self-injure have trouble forgiving themselves. Model for them that you love and forgive yourself.

A RELATIONSHIP

Emmanuel—God with us. The Christmas message is that Jesus came to earth, sent to us as a gift by the heavenly Father.

Part of God's intention in making that move was to shout the message "I'm here. I love you. I want a relationship with you." Jesus' entire earthly life was about making that relationship possible. In his death on the cross, he covered up our brokenness and our vilest wrongs, which had severed our connection with God. We need his forgiveness. Through Jesus we have it, if we ask him.

God is all about forgiveness and relationship.

As we grasp how much he has forgiven us, forgiveness of those who have hurt us most seems more and more possible. In living out our relationship with him, one that is grounded in forgiveness, we are able to begin the difficult but freeing work of forgiving both others and ourselves.

God knows forgiveness is just as important for you as it is for the person who has wronged you. Withholding it hurts you more than it hurts the person you're not forgiving. It traps you in a pool of bitterness or hate. It stagnates. It drowns. Imagine breaking through the surface of a polluted pool and inhaling a fresh, full breath of air. Forgiveness is something like that.

Emmanuel—God is with you. When you forgive, your life becomes a powerful expression of his life in you.

God, sometimes it's really hard for me to want something good for someone who has hurt me so badly. Help me begin with forgiveness. You've shown me what that looks like in how you've forgiven me. I want to understand forgiveness better, but even when I don't totally get it, help me take the beginning steps. When the hurt comes up again, remind me that I have been forgiven and can still go forward in healing from the hurt. Show me how I can begin to pray for good things for others in my life. Show me how that can help me begin to heal. AMEN.

Be kind to one another, tender-hearted, forgiving each other, just as God in Christ also has forgiven you.
EPHESIANS 4:32

GOING DEEPER

- Forgiving someone else begins with accepting God's forgiveness of you. What questions or uncertainties do you have about his forgiveness or about accepting his forgiveness of you?

- Forgiveness and relationship go together, whether in connection with God or with others. What deep hurts are holding you back from taking the first steps toward healing some of your broken relationships? What emotions?

- What good things can you begin to ask God to bring to those who have hurt you?

DEEPER STILL

Thinking about the emotions involved in forgiveness can be triggering. If you find that's the case, don't go deeply into those emotions alone. Talk about it with someone you trust, someone who knows about Jesus' forgiveness. Consider where you most struggle with forgiveness. Is it God's forgiveness of you? Your forgiveness of yourself? Your forgiveness of others?

twelve

Last night I talked to God. This morning, all morning, I've been talking to him. I told him how I was feeling sad, confused, and angry. I also told him to help me give away all I hold on to.

—Jackie's Journal

"MAKE YOURSELF AT HOME," Judy told Jackie as she smiled and waved her toward the living room. Jackie, wearing her hooded sweatshirt, walked through the dining room into the living room. The house was cozy and neat. A framed Bible verse, done in needlework, hung on one wall. It said, "Love spoken here." That was true. When she came to this home, Jackie felt love and encouragement.

She dropped down onto her usual spot on a love seat, stretched her arms toward her shaking legs, and waited. One hand clutched a folded piece of paper with a list of names on it. She could hear Judy and Stephanie finishing up in the kitchen and heading her way.

Judy handed Jackie her cup. It was her usual, her mocha.

"Thanks." Jackie took a sip and sat it on the coffee table.

Jackie had a smile for the two women as they settled into their seats. Judy chose her recliner, clicked on the nearby lamp, and pulled one leg up under her. Stephanie sat down in a chair opposite the coffee table.

Judy and Stephanie were Jackie's bosses at the bookstore where she worked. Stephanie was Judy's daughter-in-law. Both women had become friends to Jackie—and sort of like family. It was their idea to meet weekly. They thought it might help to use material they had at the store to talk and pray through the struggles that led Jackie to want to hurt herself. Maybe it would.

> She began each prayer with "Lord, I choose to forgive" and named each person and what they had done. She thought she'd never get through that night and wondered how she would get through this one.

Jackie longed to be free from cutting, and especially from the anxiety. She'd give this a try and come each week. But it was hard. Very hard.

This meeting would be especially difficult. Her list of people included those who had molested her and guys whom she had chosen to be sexually involved with. Several weeks before, she had a similar lengthy list. For that one, she began each prayer with "Lord, I choose to forgive" and named each person and what they had done. She thought she'd never get through that night and wondered how she would get through this one.

"OK, let's get started," Judy said. She pulled out some papers she used to help direct their prayer time and handed copies to Jackie and Stephanie. She turned to Jackie. "Tonight's Scriptures remind us that we need to honestly bring up the sins we have been a part of. Some of yours were your own choice, some weren't."

Jackie pulled her arms across her stomach. The nausea was setting in early tonight.

Judy began to read selected verses from the Bible. Jackie listened to the words about resisting the devil and sin, and praying and confessing our wrongs to God and to each other.

"And the last one here says, 'If we confess our sins, he is faithful and righteous to forgive us our sins and to cleanse us from all unrighteousness.' That's 1 John chapter 1, verse 9." She glanced up at Jackie. "We can't just send up a quick 'Sorry, God.' We need to tell him what we did, with true sorrow. He promises that we will receive his forgiveness. Let's go ahead and pray."

Judy lowered her head and began to pray for Jackie to be set free from all that she struggled to overcome.

" . . . and God, direct Jackie's heart to listen to you and know how she can pray for anything that has saddened you about her life." Judy paused and left time for silent prayer. Then she continued. Jackie kept her head bowed and listened as Judy read a list of different kinds of actions and thoughts that offend God.

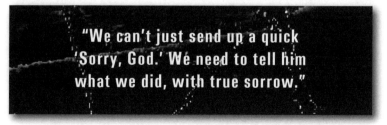

"We can't just send up a quick 'Sorry, God.' We need to tell him what we did, with true sorrow."

Jackie's thoughts seemed everywhere.

God, I'm such a big sinner. I've made many choices that I

know have messed up my relationship with you. And that doesn't even count what others have done to me.

As Stephanie and Jackie kept their heads down, Judy modeled a prayer. "Father God, I want to confess the sins I have committed. Forgive me for using my body in ways that didn't honor you or the way you created me. Thank you for forgiving me and cleansing me. Strengthen me so I can stay away from this kind of sin in the future."

Jackie lifted her head and realized Judy was waiting. "Now?" she asked.

"Yes, go ahead."

Jackie spent the next few moments talking to God and asking for his forgiveness. She finished and grew quiet. They kept their heads down.

"You understand Jesus forgives you for all those things?" Stephanie asked her.

"Yes."

Stephanie then prayed. "Jesus, Jackie has been obedient and confessed her sin. We hold to the truth that she is forgiven in your name. Help her know that in her heart."

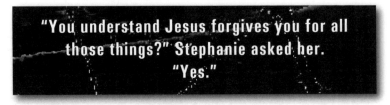

"You understand Jesus forgives you for all those things?" Stephanie asked her. "Yes."

The night went on, with more talk and sharing . . .

Judy moved on. "I know this is difficult," she said. She took a breath, then read some verses about not allowing

SCARS THAT WOUND : SCARS THAT HEAL

sin to rule your body or your choices in life, and about how important it is to see your body as a special place where the Holy Spirit lives.

Jackie guessed what was coming next. She twisted her hands together as her stomach tightened. Was she going to throw up? She turned toward Judy, who had stopped reading and was now looking at her. *What had she just said?*

"We're right here with you." Judy's voice was gentle as she urged Jackie on. "Read your list and talk to God about what happened."

"OK." Jackie unfolded the paper and looked down the list. It was long. *What if I don't do this right?* "Wait just a minute." Her chest lifted and fell with a sigh. *Is this going to help? What if thinking it all through and saying it out loud makes things worse?*

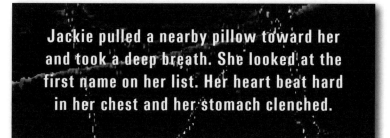

Jackie pulled a nearby pillow toward her and took a deep breath. She looked at the first name on her list. Her heart beat hard in her chest and her stomach clenched.

Judy and Stephanie were quiet. Jackie knew they'd wait until she was ready.

"OK, I'm going to do it now." Jackie pulled a nearby pillow toward her and took a deep breath. She looked at the first name on her list. Her heart beat hard in her chest and her stomach clenched. Now she was sure she would throw up any minute. She stopped and pulled her hood over her head.

I'm going to do this, God. I've talked about every one of these in counseling with John. Unless I remember something new, I can get through this.

She read the first name on the list. She prayed to be released from the horrible memories. She begged God to break all emotional connections to each person who had violated her. She asked for forgiveness for using her body in sexual ways that didn't honor the way God had made her. Finally, she prayed and accepted that God had really made her free and clean.

And then, she was done.

"Amen!" said Judy and Stephanie, almost in unison.

The two women rose from their chairs and gave Jackie a hug.

Jackie smiled. She was really shaking now. She set the pillow in its place on the sofa and took a few slow breaths. The nausea still rumbled through her stomach. She couldn't wait to get to her car. She stood and walked to the kitchen to pour out her cooled mocha. Judy and Stephanie chatted and followed her.

"Yeah, I'm OK." At least she was trying to convince her body she was.

Turning from the sink, Jackie tried to keep her mood light. "Thanks, for everything."

Stephanie gave her another hug. "I love you. You doin' OK?"

"Yeah, I'm OK." At least she was trying to convince her body she was. "See you tomorrow." Her hood still covered her head as she left the house and went out into the chilly November night.

Getting out of the house and into her car didn't seem to help calm Jackie. The quietness of the drive only punctuated her anxiety and everything she remembered about the evening. She reached the house that she shared with seven other women, but everyone was asleep. She would try to do the same. Maybe she'd begin to feel better.

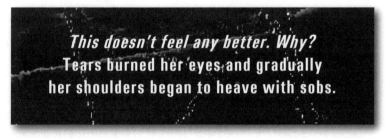

This doesn't feel any better. Why? Tears burned her eyes and gradually her shoulders began to heave with sobs.

But sleep wasn't coming. Her anxiety rose, and her mind and heart raced. Tucked in the corner of a windowsill next to her bed, she kept a package of razor blades. She sat up and slid out a blade, then made her way to the bathroom. *I wish I could get past this without turning to cutting. God, help me.*

She closed her eyes and held the blade tightly. Her whole body shook. She wanted it to stop. Could it, without her cutting herself? *It won't stop. I have to.* She cut herself once on her arm. Then again, and again, and again. There. She waited for the relaxed feeling to come.

But it didn't.

This doesn't feel any better. Why? Tears burned her eyes and gradually her shoulders began to heave with sobs. *God, I really want to stop relying on this to get me through. I want to rely on you.* As she cried, she cleaned her arm. Anxiety still trembled through her body.

She felt her way toward the dining room, where the phone was. It was late, and Judy was probably asleep, but she had to call. After several rings, Judy picked up.

Jackie took a breath to slow her sobs. "It's me—Jackie." She paused and inhaled another shaky breath. "I cut myself. I didn't feel anything this time. It didn't help. And I still feel really anxious."

"Jackie, remember all we accomplished in our prayers earlier tonight?"

"Yes."

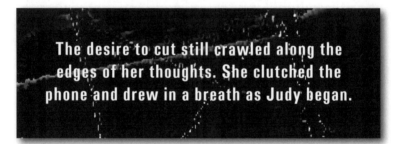

The desire to cut still crawled along the edges of her thoughts. She clutched the phone and drew in a breath as Judy began.

"God is still with you. You know, it's a good thing that cutting wasn't successful in numbing your feelings. Now you can watch him work and show you that he has begun healing you in this area. You don't need cutting anymore."

Jackie sniffed. "I don't want to need it anymore. I want to trust God."

"Can I pray for you?"

"Yes." The desire to cut still crawled along the edges of her thoughts. She clutched the phone and drew in a breath as Judy began.

"God, I want to pray right now against the enemy, Satan . . ."

Jackie battled to focus.

"Reveal the truth of who she is as your child and the freedom you have given her . . ."

As Judy's calming voice provided a little more assurance with each word, Jackie felt the anxious pounding in her chest begin to ease.

" . . . You are her only source of healing. Amen."

They both were quiet for a moment, then Judy spoke. "Do you want to come back over here tonight?"

"No, I'll be OK here." She sniffed and wiped her nose on her sleeve. "This was a hard night."

"God is working."

"I want to believe that. I really do. Thanks, Judy, for praying."

> When you are in trouble, call out to me.
> I will answer and be there to protect and honor you.
> PSALM 91:15 (CEV)

POWERFUL PRAYER

It was time. Jackie wanted to face her past and the biggest reasons why she had turned to hurting herself to begin with. She hadn't known what drove her toward self-injury at the age of fourteen.

She couldn't answer the question "Why?" Now she could. The memories were vivid and painful, the connection clear.

"I was at a point where I was ready to move on with my life," Jackie said, looking back. "I had felt stuck for so long in my bitterness and holding on to my past. I was just done. I was tired of living that way. I was thankful I had people who cared so much about me."

Though helpful, the prayer time with Judy and Stephanie had been intense. "It was scary to realize that so much abuse could happen to one person," Jackie said, looking back. "I went back to my childhood and started to think about different instances. It brought back the emotions. I remembered that I hadn't felt protected, and I began to feel hurt, sad, and angry again."

Jackie had wondered what would happen in praying. Would the prayers help? Would God think she was too awful to accept? Would she reject what he wanted for her? Jackie wrestled through her doubts but then went forward. "It's not that I thought the prayer time was going to be a quick fix, but part of me wondered if I was going to cut for the rest of my life," she said. "I realized that all God was asking me to do was be willing to trust him and follow him."

She made the decision she would trust him. She brought up event after event, and person after person. Judy said, "Some of it was really deep for Jackie, so she really wasn't aware that she was holding on to it—it still hurt, still wounded her. We wanted to pray so the enemy couldn't bring anything up and hold it against her."

Jackie remembered, "It was really hard to say the words *molest* and *rape*. It still makes me sick to say those words out loud or to read them. And then to attach those words to names was super-overwhelming."

So overwhelming that later that evening she felt the only way she could get through was to cut herself yet again. "After I was done, I felt disappointed in myself," she said. "I realized then that I didn't want to keep relying on my cutting. That night it didn't do what I wanted it to, but I also had this feeling that I just wanted to rely on the Lord. He wanted something better for me than to do that for the rest of my life."

Calling Judy was a big step. "Before that night, I had never called her for that kind of situation, but I knew she'd pray about it right then, and I wanted to bring it to the Lord. Knowing someone else knew I was struggling and having her pray for me helped me calm down."

She didn't know at the time that that night would be the last time she'd cut.

A few days later she was downstairs at the Girls' House and began to feel anxious. "I didn't even know why," she remembered later. "I started to not to be able to focus, and I started thinking about cutting, and I couldn't stop thinking about it. Usually at that point, I'd go and cut and that would take care of my obsessiveness about it. Instead, I remember thinking, I don't need to do this anymore. I think I went upstairs and made myself busy, and that started the pattern of me just not picking up the razor."

What worked best for Jackie was hanging out with people. The Girls' House had eight living there, including her. She wouldn't necessarily tell one of the others when she wanted to cut, but she'd go find where they were. "It was really easy for me to walk upstairs and hang out with whoever was around," she said. "And I called John quite a bit. We'd talk about random things. Talking stopped whatever was going on in my brain that made me want to cut."

Almost three years have passed since the night Jackie called Judy for prayer. She doesn't cut herself anymore. As she looked back to that evening, she began to realize how powerfully prayer was a part of her healing. "There's something about speaking things out loud," Jackie said. "That's one thing I learned—more spiritually—the authority we have as Christians in the spirit world. That exists, and because of Christ we already have victory."

> Before you pray with a person who self-injures, be sure you already have a solid prayer relationship with God. Prepare your own heart through prayer. Be aware of your weaknesses and God's strength in handling the relationship. Pray for wisdom and sensitivity.

RECOVERING WITH GOD

Many have experienced the same triumph over their self-injury that Jackie did.

Shauna told her story: "I tried to recover for six months without God. It was a roller coaster of doing good and then getting worse. It wasn't until I really gave it all to God that he took me out of it. One day I was deep in self-injury and the next, completely healed. Only God can do that. Self-injury is a mental struggle that the enemy uses to control your life. If you really want to be released from it, I think God has to step in and deliver you from it. That doesn't mean I don't struggle with it from time to time. It just isn't a daily thing I have to deal with."

A Web cam caught the images of Kyle cutting, and friends who saw it called rescue workers. That was a wake-up call. He realized he needed help. After a short stay in a mental hospital, Kyle attended church with a couple who were like parents to him. Kyle said that's where he "found a new relationship with God," and that included prayer. He added, "Now I know that he is always there and never leaves me." This was Kyle's beginning to recovery.

Mari had just been released from the hospital for cutting on her leg. She was sitting in her room in the dark. "I started carving. It didn't do anything," she said. "After a couple minutes, it was like I heard God talking to me about how much he loved me—no matter what, just as I am. That profoundly affected my life. God is the lover of my soul. He is there no matter what is happening around me. He never leaves me. I haven't cut since then. There have been times when I've wanted to, but didn't."

These are powerful examples of how God can work in your life. But, as in Jackie's case, dealing with overwhelming emotions, healing from past hurts, and ending your self-harming behavior may take some time—even if you're sure you honestly let God in on the process. Don't let that discourage you. Keep in mind, all these stories are true—and each is filled with a message of promise and hope. God has healing, recovery, and deliverance in mind for you.

Someone who is hurting himself may be in a beginning relationship with God and not comfortable with more than one person praying around him. Ask if it's OK. Accept fully if it's not. Ask if he'd like to pray with just one person, or use silent prayer only. Help him grow comfortable with prayer.

THE PRAYER CONNECTION

For Jackie, Mari, Shauna, and Kyle, the common ingredient in getting to a better place in their healing was their connection to God. Prayer made that possible.

Prayer is God's way for us to communicate with and be in close relationship with him. And just like most relationships, it takes some effort on our part to keep that connection going and growing. In a relationship with God, you have the added dynamic that, well, he is God—the eternal heavenly Father, God of the universe. Prayer connects you spiritually to him. That's power.

And during those times that you don't know how to begin to express what's going on inside, you have help. Romans 8:26 says, "In the same way the Spirit also helps our weakness; for we do not know how to pray as we should, but the Spirit Himself intercedes for us with groanings too deep for words." So, when you hit that kind of wall in praying, it's OK to be quiet and trust that the Holy Spirit will pray on your behalf at an unimaginable depth. You can also ask others to pray for you until you can pray to him again.

Another way to look at prayer is as a kind of battle strategy. Jackie and others have come to know all too well the aspects of the spiritual battle that include addressing deep pain and trying to fight the urges to self-harm. It's extremely tough stuff. The Bible speaks often about the enemy, Satan. He is only a fallen angel, so he will never come close to equaling God, but he can discourage and act in destructive ways in the world. In 2 Corinthians 10:3, 4, the Bible says, "For though we walk in the flesh, we do not war according to the flesh, for the weapons of our warfare are not of the flesh, but divinely powerful for the destruction of fortresses." In a relationship with God, you have access to his power, a force that will stand up to anything Satan might throw your way.

Try making prayer a regular part of your life. Step it up a couple of levels if you're already doing it. It'll take you deeper—into an amazing and powerful relationship.

God, I want a close connection to you. I want to understand how I can talk to you more and make you a part of my life every day. Help me to remember to turn to you when what I feel inside is crushing me and I want to hurt myself. This really is a battle that is way beyond me. I don't know if Satan is involved in this one, but I do know I need your help to fight the battle I'm facing right now. I want to win. With you I can. AMEN.

Give ear to my words, O Lord, consider my groaning.
Heed the sound of my cry for help, my King and my God,
for to You I pray. In the morning, O Lord,
You will hear my voice; in the morning
I will order my prayer to You and eagerly watch.

PSALM 5:1-3

GOING DEEPER

- Sometimes we struggle against the good things God has in mind for us. How might you begin to take some steps toward those things that are difficult for you to move forward in?

- Even if you've been praying for a while, you might still have questions about prayer—how it works, how to do it better. Talk through some of those questions with a friend you can trust.

- Powerful recovery is possible through a prayer relationship with God. What are a few practical ways you can make prayer a more regular part of each day?

DEEPER STILL

As Jackie faced her past, she found freedom and healing in prayer. Think about the hard situations of your past that you can bring to God—your own choices or the choices of others that hurt you. Spend time with someone who knows God well and knows how to pray, and pray together about these things.

twelve

thirteen

Jesus, I need your help today.

—Jackie's Journal

JACKIE CARRIED ANOTHER BOX into her parents' house and stacked it with others in the middle of a bedroom. As she headed back to her car for another load, she stopped outside her old bedroom and looked through the open doorway. Now the small room was storage for Dad's music equipment and the family's winter clothes.

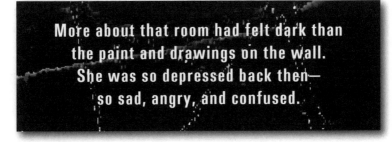

> More about that room had felt dark than the paint and drawings on the wall. She was so depressed back then— so sad, angry, and confused.

Just as well. She'd never move back in there again. Those walls were filled with memories that were hard to shake. Or to paint over. At least now the fluorescent images were gone, even if the black had proved almost impossible to cover. Jackie shivered. More about that room had felt dark than the paint and drawings on the wall. She was so depressed back then—so sad, angry, and confused.

She walked out to her car to grab a bundle of clothes. As she turned she stopped and looked at her house. A few weeks earlier, she had told Mom that before she would move back in, she wanted to pray throughout the house. She had turned to prayer more in the last few months. And not just as something religious to do. It meant a relationship with God. It meant his presence. More than anything, she wanted that in this house.

Yep. She refused to unpack one box until they had prayed.

Her boxes and belongings remained in piles for a couple more days. One evening Jackie rummaged through her stuff and found one of the prayers she had saved from the meetings with Stephanie and Judy. She headed for the living room where, she guessed, Mom was probably watching a home design program on TV.

> She no longer identified with that girl. She hadn't cut since Judy prayed with her on the phone the night after that difficult meeting.

"I wanted to show you this." Jackie handed her mom the page. "It's one of the prayers I told you about on the phone."

Mom read over the prayer and glanced up at Jackie. "Why don't we pray for the house now?"

"Do you think Dad will want to do it too?"

Mom pushed herself up off the couch. "Let's go see."

The two of them headed down the hall to find Dad in the back bedroom. He jumped at the idea. "Yeah, let's do it."

Dad started the prayer off at the front door and living room, and then they took turns throughout the rest of the house. Over

SCARS THAT WOUND : SCARS THAT HEAL

the next hour, they moved from one room to another, beginning with reading the typed prayer and then launching into their own personal words to God.

Jackie volunteered to pray in her old bedroom. As they stood inside the tiny, packed room, she remembered how there used to be a drawn stick figure on the wall—it was a girl with a gun pointing to her head. Words next to it had said, "Screaming in silence." She no longer identified with that girl. She hadn't cut since Judy prayed with her on the phone the night after that difficult meeting.

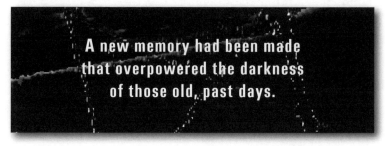

A new memory had been made that overpowered the darkness of those old, past days.

Her parents bowed their heads while Jackie recited the written prayer and asked God for safety and protection. Then Jackie prayed her thoughts. "God, help Mom feel valued. Help us show her love and respect. Thank you for who she is and how strong she is. And God, help Dad become stronger in you. Give him strength to resist drugs and alcohol. Unite us as a family. Help us become a family that is deeply rooted in you. Amen."

Dad took his turn, then Mom. They each thanked God for how far he had brought each member of their family, especially Jackie. The three smiled at each other as they stood in Jackie's old room.

A new memory had been made that overpowered the darkness of those old, past days.

Jackie stood in the middle of her new bedroom. After the day when she and her parents had prayed through the house, she had taped Bible verses, prayers, and praise songs around her room. They reminded her that God loved her, and he would help her through any battles she faced.

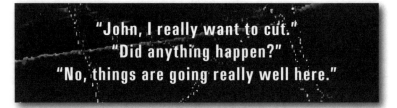

"John, I really want to cut."
"Did anything happen?"
"No, things are going really well here."

Right now, she needed that.

"I want to cut so bad," she said out loud.

The feeling wasn't new. Sometimes she still struggled with thinking she needed to cut—or just wanted to for no clear reason. So far she'd gotten past those urges. This time it stuck.

Jackie stood and paced her room. The feeling wasn't going away. She picked up her cell phone and called John. Thankfully, he answered.

"John, I really want to cut."

"Did anything happen?"

"No, things are going really well here."

"Why don't you go talk to your mom?"

"No. I remember what happened when I did that before."

"It's been a long time. Maybe she'll react differently. She seems willing to be a support for you."

"I can't tell her."

They talked a little while longer, until she had nothing more to say.

"Thanks, John."

"Let me know how it goes, OK?"

"OK." She hung up the phone.

She was *not* going to talk to Mom, but how would she get past this urge? She paced her room and felt her anxiety driving her desire to cut. Finally, she walked toward the kitchen, where Mom was doing dishes. She stood near the counter and watched her for a moment. *OK, maybe I can try.*

"Mom, I don't really know why I'm feeling this way, but I want to cut. I don't think I should be by myself."

Her mom stopped and turned toward her. "OK."

"It's just something that I need to get through."

"I'll stay with you then." Her mom paused a moment. "Why don't you help me finish the dishes?"

They hung out for the rest of the evening and watched TV. When it got late, and Jackie wanted to sleep, Mom stayed with her through the night. When morning came, Jackie still felt uneasy.

"I don't know how I'll do being by myself."

"That's OK. I'll stay home." Mom went to the phone and called in to work. She let them know she'd be in later.

By late morning, Jackie began to feel she was doing better. She told her mom she'd be fine by herself.

Mom held her keys in her hand, ready to head out the door. "Are you sure, Jackie? I can stay if you need me to."

"I'm sure."

After her mom left, Jackie kept busy cleaning the house and doing homework. Later in the afternoon, she called John and let him know she had made it through the night, and day, without cutting.

Excitement played along the edges of her voice. "My mom stayed with me the whole time," she told John. "She was totally different than I thought she'd be. It really helped to have her here with me."

Changes had never felt so good.

> "Go home to your family and tell them how much the Lord has done for you and how good he has been to you."
>
> MARK 5:19 (CEV)

GOING HOME

Five years had passed since Jackie first left home, beaten down by her past and trapped in a dangerous, downward spiral. Though she visited her parents many times during the years she was away, now she wanted to move home—at least for a little while. She wanted to make new memories; she only hoped they'd be good ones.

"The whole time I lived at the Ranch," Jackie recalled, "I didn't like that I had left home on such negative terms. I always wanted to have the experience of the natural process of a child leaving home." She also hoped that by going home, her mother and father could become a part of what God was doing in her life. "I was getting all this healing and all this good stuff was happening to me. I wanted them to see, on a daily basis, how much I had grown. I wanted them to have a part in that."

Jackie's mom was more than happy to have her return. "I remember being so excited because, when she left to get help, there hadn't been good closure to her spending the last years of her youth at home. I had a desire in my heart that she could come back and live here."

They had already discussed praying together through the house, but one night before Jackie came, her mom felt an urgency to pray at that moment. "There was always a darkness in her room," Betty said. "I prayed all night long about every crack and crevice in the house. It was like the darkness was lifted away."

Then, after Jackie arrived, the three of them prayed together in a way they never had before. That time powerfully impacted each of them. Said Jackie, "It was really emotional and so awesome. I had never experienced anything like that with my parents before." Fred, Jackie's dad, agreed. "It was a beautiful time—especially Jackie being real strong and confident in the Lord and in herself."

The prayer time launched their family into a powerful new beginning. "We were all healthier and happier, more like a normal family that talked and laughed together," Betty said. "We made a commitment to pray every night. It didn't happen every night, but we prayed together quite a bit."

In the weeks ahead, Jackie saw changes she had only dreamed might happen. "Coming home and having that prayer time opened up a lot of communication between us. I was more open and honest with them than I had ever been in my entire life," she said. "That's when my dad stopped smoking weed permanently. We went to a Christian recovery group together, which I thought he'd never go to."

Fred added, "That was a significant time. It was good for both of us—for the whole family actually. I was finally seeking help. I needed it and was afraid to let people know I was still dabbling with pot. Since then I've been clean. The Lord has been super. He keeps blessing us over and over—at church, with brothers at work—it's been really cool."

Living at home went well for Jackie, though she sometimes still struggled with wanting to cut. If she saw a knife or razor blade around the house, she had to make deliberate choices to walk by instead of picking it up and using it as she might have before. She'd distract herself by getting busy with some type of housework, cleaning, watching a TV program, or hanging out with someone. The day when the desire overwhelmed her, she discovered support in her mom that she had never felt before. "It was really different to talk to my mom about it and let her know what was really going on," Jackie said. "I tended to try and act like everything was OK so she didn't worry." It was a big step for Jackie to let her mom know she was having a hard time getting through the latest temptation, but she was glad she did. "She didn't need to know why, just, 'How can I help you?' I felt so happy and loved that she stayed with me. It meant the world to me."

Jackie also found that her relationship with her father was getting better. "I think things began to really change when I started to let him know how he affected the way I thought about myself and how important his role as a father was to me.

Around that time he was beginning to be more sensitive to what was going on with me."

Nikki was still a resident at the Ranch during this time. She was taking her own courageous steps toward change. Jackie lived with her parents for eight months before moving back to live closer to her Ranch family and friends. She missed them and decided to return to the area and continue her education. But the time at home would be forever set in her heart as being right on the edge of miraculous.

If there had been any potential for regret, it would only have been from never having attempted it.

> Someone who self-injures may continue to struggle with believing people really want to understand her. Take a close look at your communication. Are you showing an interest and concern in her life and what she thinks and feels?

Realistic Hopes

The changes that Jackie and her family experienced hadn't come quickly or easily. No matter how difficult, Jackie had to be willing to go forward in her own healing, even if nothing changed with others around her. And then as the changes became evident, she had to be realistic. God still had plenty of work to do—in everyone.

Hopes about your family can seem huge and out of reach. Though Alisa saw that her dad was trying to be loving, she still hoped for more resolution in their relationship. "I still pray for changes," she said. "My dad is not saved. He still does drugs and has never asked for forgiveness for hurting me."

Counselor Susan Cook reminds those who feel discouraged about family relationships not changing to see the bigger picture of their life and the many seasons ahead where those relationships can be revisited. "You don't have to choose 'forever' right now," she tells her clients.

Some things may not change. That doesn't mean that you have to stay stuck with those who refuse to move forward. You can grow and change. Others may be inspired and change too, or they may never understand or see it. Either way, you can decide to keep the forward motion because it matters for your life.

As Dan understood more about why he self-injured, he knew he needed to accept responsibility for it. "I realized that while I was hurt by others, I still make the decision to harm myself," he said. "Nobody is forcing me to do it. Sometimes we want to say that we self-injure because of something that happened to us and, to a large extent, that's true. But I believe that we also have the ability to choose how to respond to the actions of others."

He's right. Nobody can take that choice from you. And no one can keep you from heading in a better direction for yourself. That past that feels like chains around your feet? Step out of those shackles and go forward. You'll be making better memories to look back on—ones that can begin to outshine any of the hurts from your past.

Mari looked back and saw where God had shown up in her life. She now feels confident that he'll keep working. "Sometimes I remember how I used to be in the past and (see) how far I've come," she said. "When I feel like I'm spinning my wheels or that things are too stressful, God reminds me of when I couldn't even go outside without panic attacks, or of when I had trouble even talking to other people. Then I look at my friends that I have now. I am slowly opening myself up to others. That is a big step for me. By remembering these things, I know that I'm not alone. Life is a process and I'm slowly growing into what God has planned for me."

Shauna, who self-harmed through cutting and an eating disorder, found that looking back doesn't always have to be focused on what was painful. "Remembering the good things God has done in my life is something I do often to encourage me to move forward," she said. "I remember all the times I experienced his presence, the times he healed me or someone I know."

Remembering the good things—Shauna and Mari might be on to something.

> It's very possible that the person who self-injures feels that others have let him down. In some way, you may have done so, even if you didn't intend to. Be willing to talk through anything he might be feeling.

THINKING ABOUT THE GOOD STUFF

Encouraging remembrances has always been a big deal to God. You can read in the Bible how often he asked the Israelites to set up a memorial or observe a regular feast to remember something good that had happened because of his presence, protection, or provision. God knows that it's pretty much human nature to grumble and focus on the negative, and especially to forget about the good things. So he encouraged the Israelites: "Remember."

The apostle Paul, one of the main writers in the New Testament, knew of that human tendency too. In writing to the Philippians, he encouraged them, in their prayers and requests to God, to think of the things they could be thankful for. He went on and gave them a fantastic list of good thoughts to fill their minds with: "Summing it all up, friends, I'd say you'll do best by filling your minds and meditating on things true, noble, reputable, authentic, compelling, gracious—the best, not the worst; the beautiful, not the ugly; things to praise, not things to curse" (Philippians 4:8, *The Message*).

Think about the good stuff. Look back in your life and see where God showed up. Remembering in this way is encouraging. It sets your mind toward what has gone well— instead of being all about what hasn't.

> *God, sometimes it doesn't feel like I have much control over what's going through my mind, but I have more of a choice than I sometimes have thought. As I remember back, help me to see the signs of where you worked in my life and where you worked through others and showed your love for me. Each day help me think less about the things that make me angry or anxious, and more about what is true and good and worthy of praising you.* AMEN.

> I remember the days of long ago; I meditate on all
> your works and consider what your hands have done.
>
> PSALM 143:5 (NIV)

GOING DEEPER

■ Sometimes it's hard to think of anything good when everything seems to be going so wrong. Keep digging. What is in your past that has been the best instead of the worst?

■ Look closely. You might see where God showed up even when you didn't know it. Where do you think he might have been with you, working in your life?

■ Remembering or filling your mind with the good stuff changes your outlook on what lies ahead. Spend a few minutes coming up with the longest list you can of what you like about your past, your present, about you, and about God.

DEEPER STILL

God thinks memorials are a great idea. Think of something you can create—a sculpture, a poem, a song, a drawing, maybe something as simple as a verse or saying painted on a rock—to help you remember the good things he has been doing in your life. If you like gardening, plant a tree.

fourteen

It's nice to tell people I've had a good day.

—Jackie's Journal

JACKIE WAS ONCE AGAIN IN MIKE'S OFFICE at the Ranch. Today she sat on the sofa cushion nearest to his chair. On that August day a few years before, she had worn long sleeves and all black clothes. This September day was just as warm, and she wore shorts and a tank top.

> "Sometimes I look at the role you and John have played in my life. I want that kind of relationship with my dad."

"You and John have been like fathers to me." She brushed tears from her eyes and laughed. "Sorry. I'm being emotional." She took in a breath, blew it out slowly, then laughed again. She let out a sigh. "You've been so awesome and encouraging to me. I missed you guys while I was gone. Sometimes I look at the role you and John have played in my life. I want that kind of relationship with my dad. I just don't think it's ever going to happen."

Mike leaned back in his chair and put his hands behind his head. "Wouldn't it be great if that relationship existed someday?"

"Yeah, it would."

"In order for it to happen, he'd have to be open and honest with you, show you some of the simple expressions of patience and approval you've received here."

Jackie nodded. She wanted that more than anything. Tears escaped, falling down her cheeks.

"Well, why don't we pray for it?"

"OK."

They bowed their heads for prayer . . .

The next evening, Jackie visited her friends at the Girls' House. As she sliced some fruit, she thought about her plans for the evening.

"I'm going to miss *CSI* tonight," she said out loud, some disappointment in her voice.

At her parents' house she had watched the show faithfully with her dad. She could ask him to record it for her, she thought. She set the knife down and went to the phone to call. Dad answered right away.

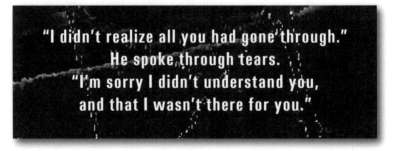

"I didn't realize all you had gone through." He spoke through tears. "I'm sorry I didn't understand you, and that I wasn't there for you."

"Hey Dad, I'm not going to be able to watch *CSI* tonight. Can you record it for me?" Silence hung between them. "Dad?"

His answer was quiet. "You made me cry today."

Was she in trouble? Had he found one of her journals and read something she'd written a long time ago? "What did I do?"

"I read your testimony in the church newsletter."

She let out a sigh of relief. A few weeks before, the staff at her old church had asked Jackie to write part of her story. They published it in the newsletter, but she hadn't shown it to Dad yet.

"I didn't realize all you had gone through." He spoke through tears. "I'm sorry I didn't understand you, and that I wasn't there for you." After another short silence he went on. "I know it was the drugs and alcohol. I was a total jerk. I'm sorry. I'm so sorry."

Tears streamed down Jackie's face. "It's OK, Dad."

"I'm so proud of you, Jackie. I love you."

"I love you too, Dad."

Answer me, O Lord, for Your lovingkindness is good;
According to the greatness of Your compassion, turn to me.

PSALM 69:16

ANOTHER PRAYER ANSWERED

"I called my dad, and we had the best conversation." Jackie was pumped up to share the news with her friends.

Before that phone call, Jackie and her father rarely talked on the phone. When they did, their conversations stayed on the basics—the latest news, what they each were doing. Nothing too personal. "This one was real—real feelings," Jackie said. "It wasn't all masks. I felt like we connected on a deeper level."

Her story's appearance in the church newsletter helped prompt that depth. Jackie's dad was aware of her writing the story but hadn't seen it until he got his copy. "I sat down and read the whole thing and I was in tears," Fred said. In those moments, he realized how unaware he had been of how Jackie's rape had affected her and how much she had turned to drugs and self-injury. "I didn't know she had suffered so much. I thought, 'Oh, Lord Jesus, how could I have helped her then?' I asked him for forgiveness." When Jackie called that night he took the opportunity to tell her what he felt. "I wanted to tell her how much I loved her and how sorry I was—not being the greatest dad back then."

That conversation is still a highlight for Jackie. "I just wanted to listen," she remembered. "I was focused because I wanted to hear what he had to say. I kept saying, 'It's OK.' And I really felt that. I had forgiven him. At this point, I felt confident in my healing without my parents, so this was like a bonus—wow!"

They ended their talk that night by joking and having some fun. She was finally having a conversation with her dad in ways she'd always hoped she could. It felt good. Now the two of them talk on the phone all the time, she said.

She no longer feels scared of her dad or put down by him. "We have more of a father-daughter relationship," Jackie said. "I feel loved and encouraged by him. And I think I've come to a place where I allow him to be who he is, and I don't hold him up to this high standard. His expectations of me are better too. We just enjoy where we're at."

Jackie and her family continue to grow in their relationships with each other and with God. "Our relationships are definitely a lot healthier," she said. "We communicate better. I'm no longer assuming they should know how I'm doing just because they're my parents. We've all really grown in the Lord as a family. I enjoy being around them."

> Make verbal encouragement a regular part of your time spent with someone who self-injures. It's possible that kind of support has been lacking in her life.

JACKIE TODAY

Jackie's past experiences left her feeling like she wasn't worth anyone's time. "I always felt invaluable—sometimes like I was a cheap whore," she said. "That's really starting to change. I want better for myself. I see myself having good relationships with people, and hopefully with a future husband. I always envisioned myself with someone who's going to hurt me—like I deserved that. Now I see myself with someone who's going to respect me and care about me."

Jackie has made huge strides in her view of God, herself, and others. Her life has become an encouragement to many. Melody, Jackie's youth leader, said, "I am still amazed at the mature level that Jackie has reached at her still-young age, and her ability to see things through a different perspective than a lot of people do. She has a great ability for forgiveness. I see a young woman who has a very bright future."

Stephanie, one of the managers at the bookstore where Jackie worked, said, "She is certainly happier. Her confidence is going strong. For me personally, I feel I can trust her. She not only works for us in our store, but she's there for us as a family. I see her as understanding who she is, that she is definitely loved by God, and that she has a purpose. She has a confidence that she's not just someone who is always needing help—*she* can help someone else who is struggling. She builds relationships and friendships and is giving of her time. Definitely a loving person."

Now approaching her late twenties, Jackie has pursued her dream of training to work in the medical field. When she walked into the classroom the first day, she wore short sleeves and let the scars on her arms show. "I've never started a new place without long sleeves," she said. "And if I forgot to wear long sleeves, I've usually hidden my arms under the tables. That time I was just sitting there like anyone else. Cutting, and even my scars, don't consume my life anymore."

In class, and in other places, people do notice Jackie's scars. Sometimes she's aware that they are looking at her arms instead of her face. "A couple years ago I couldn't handle wearing short sleeves and people staring at my arms. Now when little things like that happen, I think of how far I've come."

A very long ways. Her journey out of self-injury was one of many changes and victories in her life. Even when she struggled to believe, God was with her every moment. He worked in her heart, increasing her faith in him, and he worked through others, reminding her of his love.

Thinking beyond today or next week can be difficult for someone who self-harms. Look for an opportunity to talk about dreams and wishes for the future. Help him see how they can be possible.

In Jackie's life and in the lives of each of those who have chosen to trust God, he works in ways far beyond even what we can conceive of. As Ephesians 3:20 says, God "is able to do immeasurably more than all we ask or imagine" (*NIV*).

Some of the others whose stories were shared in this book also shared the ways they'd like to see God busting the boundaries of their imaginations:

> I want a closer relationship with God. I want to be able to be open and honest in my relationships and allow people to really get to know me. — *Mari*

> I hope that I'll continue to grow in overcoming my self-injury. I'm more alert to the situations and feelings that trigger it, and I know that I can choose a different path than self-harm. With help from God and others, I believe I can do it. — *Dan*

> I've come a long way in really knowing how to deal with my thoughts, working through them, and knowing where to go with them. I hope God can give me the strength to reach out to other people who go through the same thing, and that I can give them what I would have wanted when I was going through it. — *Jena*

> My goal is to never hurt myself again, and to believe in myself. — *Ericka*

> I hope that some day I'll be able to stop cutting and stop getting the urges. I also hope that one day I'll be able to help others with their cutting and support them and help them heal. — *Ryan*

fourteen

I plan to teach high school. I look forward to what God has in store for me once I start teaching and to see what else he has waiting for me in the future. — *Callie*

I want to be able to continue to build my relationship with God and to continue to mature so I'm better equipped to deal with whatever life hands me. I also want to be able to share my life experiences and knowledge of God with others who are in the same situation I'm recovering from. — *Kyle*

I just really want God to use my story to help others who are stuck in the dark world of self-injury. I want them to see the light at the end of the tunnel and find God. God has given me the compassion to love them where they are and help lead them to a place of healing. — *Shauna*

I no longer want to hurt myself to get rid of the pain or to control my life in some way. I go to the cross. I have a deep appreciation for the concept that our bodies are the temple of the Holy Spirit. I have a desire to share—with others who hurt or have hurt themselves in this way—the truth about our bodies and about the help and healing Jesus offers them. — *Suzy*

Colossians 3:2 says, "Set your mind on the things above, not on the things that are on earth." Through your relationship with Christ you are connected to the vastness of God's grace and power. "Setting your mind on things above" is thinking beyond the boundaries of yourself toward all that life in him is or can be.

"Setting your mind on things above" also is reaching toward and claiming everything God has in mind for you—what he has promised to do that is far beyond anything you could ask for or dream of. It's deciding you're ready and determined to live your life, not in a deep pit or even in status quo—but fully and abundantly. In John 10:10, Jesus said this of his followers, who he affectionately referred to as his sheep: "The thief comes only to steal and kill and destroy; I came that they may have life, and have it abundantly."

Don't let anything steal or destroy the fullness of life God wants you to have. With him, your future can bust the boundaries of your imagination. Your scars and wounds can be healed.

Go for it.

God, give me the ability to think beyond the boundaries of myself to the amazing fullness of life you have for me. I'm ready to journey with you out of my self-injury. I'm ready to look toward a future that is beyond anything I can imagine. Help me walk that journey in faith. Thank you that you are with me now and will be with me every step I take. AMEN.

From the fullness of his grace we have all received one blessing after another.
JOHN 1:16 (NIV)

GOING DEEPER

■ God's power and grace in your life are huge gifts. Take a moment to think about all you know about who he is and the limitlessness of that grace and power in healing you from self-injury.

■ Living by the status quo or living life to the full: What could be the differences between the two in your life?

■ Just like Jackie, you're on a journey. How do you see God working to increase your faith and to involve others in your healing? How might you invite more of that?

DEEPER STILL

In your journal, make a list of what you'd like to see happen in your future. Turn it into a prayer. When you're done, remember that what God plans for you is far beyond anything you wrote down—really, beyond anything you could think to ask or imagine.

A LETTER FROM JACKIE

WHEN I FIRST STARTED CUTTING, self-injury was something that not many had heard about. I felt so alone and wished there was someone who understood where I was coming from and who could help me. I didn't feel that many were going to be able to do those things. As hard as it was talking about my life for this book and having to remember a lot of painful stuff, I've prayed that the Lord will use it to point others in the right direction.

Cutting consumed my life. I thought about when I was going to be able to cut next, where I was going to cut, and how deep I would go. Then I thought about how I was going to hide the cuts. What if people saw? What would I tell them? I became obsessed with the thought of cutting. I felt my world might end if I couldn't do it. I wondered if I was ever going to stop or if it would be something I'd have to deal with for the rest of my life.

Every time I cut, I felt like a failure: why, after all these years, was I still doing it? As I learned more about myself, I realized it made me relaxed and calm. All the emotions I hated feeling, like anger and anxiety, were gone for a moment. That's all I wanted. It was really hard to give that up. I had spent much of my life running and escaping. The thought of dealing with life on my own was scary.

I began to realize I wasn't alone, and that I didn't have to deal with life on my own. The Lord had brought people into my life who loved me and cared about me. I had to be willing to accept their love and help and try different things to overcome the cutting. That willingness, and my willingness to trust the Lord, started my recovery.

To go from having something like this consume your life for so long and then look back and realize you haven't done it for a few years is mind-blowing. I really couldn't have done it without the relationships in my life and my relationship with Jesus.

It has taken a lot of talking and being open and honest with people and with myself, and a lot of energy, to have the life I have today. The Lord is faithful. He's the one person who will always be there for you when the rest of the world isn't.

If you are in a spot that seems hopeless and dark, know that it can get better. You can feel hope again. Remember, it's a process. It's not something that happens overnight. Jesus is your strength. He will see you through.

Jackie

A LETTER FROM JAN

As I wrote this book, the faces of young people who self-injure would come to my mind—and not always those I've met. Many times as I wrote a section, one face would come into focus for me, and the writing became very purposeful and personal. I sometimes wept, much as I did at times when I met with Jackie or when I read her journals, or when I heard the stories of others who shared with me so honestly.

I thought often of you, the reader. I prayed that somewhere in these pages you'd find words that could offer you some fresh hope; and words that would connect you more solidly with Jesus and with others who could help you tell your own story and accompany you on your journey out of self-injury.

I won't stop praying for that.

I also pray for you the prayer of Ephesians 3:17-19: "That Christ may dwell in your hearts through faith; and that you, being rooted and grounded in love, may be able to comprehend with all the saints what is the breadth and length and height and depth, and to know the love of Christ which surpasses knowledge, that you may be filled up to all the fullness of God."

Keep that fullness and power in sight. Don't ever give up.

Jan

ABOUT THE AUTHOR

JAN KERN WRITES AND SPEAKS from her passion to know God deeply, as well as from her personal journey of struggle, loss, pain, and questioning. For more than twenty-five years, she has worked with ministries and groups with which she has had the privilege of mentoring and encouraging teens, young adults, and parents.

She and her husband, Tom, live and work at a residential ranch for at-risk youth, ages sixteen to twenty-four, where Jan enjoys fostering friendships with the residents and college interns who serve there. And Jan and Tom will drop just about anything when their adult children, Dan and Sarah, come for visits to their home tucked in the foothills of the California Sierras.

Want to drop Jan a note or reach her for a speaking engagement? Contact her at:

www.choose2livefree.com

RESOURCES

The Web

WWW.CHOOSE2LIVEFREE.COM is a Christian site for teens and young adults. Up-to-date Web resources and links for issues, including self-injury, can be accessed through the site's resources page. This is a site to visit frequently and join others in keeping inspired to *live free.*

WWW.ALPINECONNECTION.ORG is Christian Hill's site for his Colorado Springs-based counseling center. The site includes an excellent brochure about self-injury.

WWW.SELF-INJURY.ORG is a Christian site offered by someone who has been there. It is packed with information, resources, and links for those who self-injure and those who support them in their recovery.

Books

No More Pain!: Breaking the Silence of Self-Injury—The author tells her personal experience with self-injury while encouraging readers that understanding and recovery are possible. Christian faith-based. As a caution, some parts of the book can be triggering.
Written by Vicki F. Duffy, Xulon Press, 2004.

See My Pain!: Creative Strategies and Activities for Helping Young People Who Self-Injure—The writers offer a variety of creative strategies and activities to help children and adolescents who self-injure. The ideas can be used by individuals or in groups.
Written by Susan Bowman, EdS, LPC, and Kaye Randall, LMSW, YouthLight, Inc., 2005.

The Scarred Soul: Understanding & Ending Self-Inflicted Violence—This has been a popular pick since its release in 1997. It includes helpful information and resources with a useful workbook-style approach. I recommend this book be read with someone—a counselor, pastor, or support person—while keeping in mind the concepts within *Scars That Wound : Scars That Heal*, and the essential role of faith needed for total freedom and healing from self-injury.
Written by Tracy Alderman, New Harbinger Publications, 1997.

Way to Live: Christian Practices for Teens—Written mostly by teens, this book is packed with personal stories and creative ways to deepen your awareness of God's presence in your life. It's included here as an example of the kinds of books that are out there to keep you busy and engaged in developing your faith while you're healing from self-injury.
Edited by Dorothy C. Bass and Don C. Richter, Upper Room Books, 2002.

An excerpt . . .

the trap

"A BUNCH OF US ARE HANGING OUT over at Nate's. You and Kaela want to come?"

Hearing Matt's voice made Suzy's heart skip a beat. Their relationship was over after someone saw her at a party making out with one of Matt's friends, and then word got back to Matt. Totally stupid. It didn't mean anything, but it ended things with him. But then they didn't have much going for them in their relationship anyway. At least he wasn't mad anymore or he wouldn't be calling.

"Just a sec. Let me ask Kaela." Suzy put her hand over her phone and checked to see what her friend wanted to do. Kaela was usually up for anything. Suzy told her what the guys were asking. Kaela, lying on Suzy's bedroom floor and flipping through an issue of *Teen* magazine, didn't hesitate.

Suzy uncovered the phone. "Sure."

"OK, Josh and I will come pick you up."

As the four of them walked into Nate's house, Suzy noticed some of Matt's other friends sitting around the den. Open bottles of alcohol and half-empty glasses sat on the counter and coffee table. No other girls? Guess it didn't matter. They were just hanging out. Nate's mom passed through. They might as well have been invisible. She didn't seem to care what they were doing.

"How's it going?" Josh grinned somewhat shyly at Suzy. "You want some Jose Cuervo?"

"What?"

"Tequila."

She'd try anything once . . . or twice. "Sure." She sat down on the couch near Josh as he handed her the bottle. No glass? She shrugged. Suzy tipped her head back and took in a mouthful of the clear liquid. It burned going down, but also tasted sweet and strong.

She heard laughter and turned to see Kaela falling into the lap of one of the guys. As she watched the scene, she felt her head growing lighter. She laughed too. When she turned back, Josh was sitting closer, leaning toward her. She could smell the alcohol on his breath. She sipped more of the tequila and watched the scene around her. Everyone was getting drunk. A distant caution pricked at her thoughts, but it blurred quickly and was gone.

Josh put his arms around her and kissed her neck. It was now easy to give in and respond. She slid into his lap. As she did, she heard Matt's slurred voice in her ear: "You'll be Josh's first."

She looked up and Matt was gone, but she saw Kaela and her guy laughing and tripping down the hallway toward the bedrooms.

Then Josh was standing and pulling her up with him. The room spun as he drew her toward the hallway. She followed.

The next moments swirled by in a mixture of tequila dizziness and sex. His first but not hers—that was gone. Even in her light-headed state, she felt sadness welling deep inside. She had lied about her self-inflicted injuries, and some believed she had been raped. The lie had taken on life and spread. So now she was marked. *Why not make it all true? Punish myself for telling it . . . like going to Matt's that day.* The thought startled her: *Am I punishing myself? Could that be part of the reason I had sex with Matt?* Her heart wrenched and she groaned.

She sat up, and her stomach pitched. Josh was leaving the room. Where was he going? As she began pulling on her jeans, she noticed that Matt was now in front of her.

"I'm next." There appeared to be a lazy smile on his face as he pushed her back onto the bed. Her soul cried and then fell silent as Matt took his turn with her. At moments she felt the battle inside. *You deserve better. No . . . you don't—this is what you chose.*

The time passed in hazy emotional agony. She tried to shut down the internal accusations, and found herself detaching to survive. *It doesn't matter. It's only sex. It doesn't mean anything. I don't mean anything.*

She heard muffled voices on the other side of the closed door—arguing.

Matt rolled off the bed and started to dress.

She pulled on her clothes and opened the door.

Kaela was there, grabbing Suzy's arm. "Let's go."

Suzy was still plenty buzzed. "Why? What's—?"

"We're going right *now*." Kaela was mad. "Matt, take us home."

When the two got back to Suzy's house, she wanted to know what had gotten Kaela so hot.

"What ticked me off? You should have—" She heaved a sigh. "Oh, forget it. If you don't . . ."

"Tell me. What happened? Did someone hurt you?"

"Nothing happened to *me*. Don't you know what was going on there?" Kaela was steaming. "If you had stayed, every one of those guys would have ended up in that room with you."

Suzy drew in a quick breath and sat down on her bed. Kaela stood there with arms crossed. Suzy began to grasp what was going on behind that glare. "You stopped them, didn't you?"

"*Yes*, I stopped them."

Suzy steadied herself, her mind beginning to free itself of the tequila. Closing her eyes, she let her head drop back. She saw it now. Josh, then Matt, then—what would have been next? *Who* would have been next? She shook her head, swallowed. She deserved it. She'd made that first choice with Matt only weeks ago. Then every date or party since involved someone with those kinds of expectations—not sex, but not far from it either. That's how they saw her now—easy. This isn't at all what she wanted when she started going after that new image.

She felt nauseated and it had nothing to do with the alcohol. She looked at Kaela still standing there, seething. Suzy looked away and flinched at the pain in her heart.

She'd have to shut that down before she crumbled.

**Free me from the trap that is set for me,
for you are my refuge.**

Psalm 31:4

A shell. An object. A toy.

That's how Suzy now saw her body. So that's how she thought guys saw her. She used her body to get attention, to be accepted. They used her body for sex.

No one thought of the person who was dying inside.

She really did begin to feel like just an object to be used by others. "I was only skin deep. Sex meant nothing to me anymore," Suzy remembered later. And changing her course didn't cross her mind. "I was so given into that lifestyle at that point—I don't know—I wasn't looking at the consequences. I wasn't able to. And that's a really dangerous place. It snowballed for me really easily."

She remembers that season of her life with deep sadness and still some shame. "I walked into a lifestyle where the more I did it, the less I cared about myself, and the more I wanted to beat myself up and give more of myself away."

"I gave myself away"—those words get used a lot. For Suzy, they have deep meaning. "God has forgiven me, but now I'm married and sometimes I think back to the situations I put myself in. And because I have those memories, because they are a part of me, it forever changed my life, forever affected me. When I'm ninety I will still have those memories. People don't realize that. They don't realize how permanent those kinds of decisions are. You can't get that innocence back."

She knows. The forgiveness Suzy has experienced is very real—but so are the memories.

God's design for sex needs to be openly discussed. There needs to be more to the message than "sex before marriage is wrong." Read about it. Study it in the Bible. Communicate its importance. Live it out with conviction.

HONORING

Being molested a couple of times when she was little led Suzy to view herself in distorted ways. She had come to see sex only as something you do, or something that is done to you. It didn't have much meaning beyond that. But that view is so far from God's intention for sex—an expression of love within marriage, a bonding with one person, a part of enjoying getting to know one person intimately in every way. Suzy had no idea that sex was a gift for two people to enjoy, an intimacy without shame.

When sex is used in other ways, eventually it's going to feel empty and unsatisfying. It would be some time before Suzy would fully grasp that her body and emotions were crying out for her to stop. Her hope is that others won't walk the same path she did, but if they do, that they can find a way back. "There are girls out there who have been used and have let themselves be treated that way, and now they feel like trash. They need to know there's hope, healing, forgiveness—life after the state they've been in. Newness."

Many do find that newness. Nicole, who was sexually abused from age three and then became sexually active at seventeen, is finding healing through learning her worth in God's sight. She said, "I'm learning how to share my heart and my mind more and seeing that that is valuable." And she is finding, in a current relationship, that her boundaries can be respected and that she is still loved.

Grasp the gift and value of sex as God intended it. Grab hold of the truth of your personal value. You're worth much more than just being used as an object. You're worth the beautiful, mysterious, and sacred gift of a union that God has for you and your future spouse.

And it's not just about self. When we keep in mind God's intention and timing for sex, we know that others are worth honoring, not violating in any way. Sex before marriage *always* dishonors the other person. Dressing to attract and to stir up emotions and hormones, touching, talking, inviting sexual thoughts or activities—all dishonor.

Stephanie learned at a young age that her femininity had power. "It became an art for me to hook guys and use them to meet my needs," she said. "I didn't think of them and how my behavior affected their spirit and soul."

Another way to think of it is to consider that the other person is someone's future spouse. Check yourself. Consider your words, actions, behavior, and thoughts toward the opposite sex. Every bit of it matters. If you're crossing lines and not honoring that person, it's a problem.

It's a lot about watching ourselves to see if we're being selfish and using someone else for our own pleasure. We could call it "exploiting," because essentially that's what it is.

Ryan, who was raised with the belief that he needed to get out there and have sex, has learned to see women very differently. "When I look at a girl, instead of looking at her with lust, I remember she is a child of God, just as I am. She is worth something and special to God. I don't see her as an object of just 'easy fun.'"

When you begin to see yourself and others differently—the way God views us—it will impact the situations you choose to be in, how you honor yourself, and how you honor someone else. It's a great discovery.

> Capture an honoring mentality and be an example to others. How do you treat the opposite sex? How do you dress? How do you talk to them or about them? Do you honor them as Christ would?

'LOVE AND HONOR' NOW

"Treat others with respect." It's a common phrase. But the thing is, we don't always do that. There's something about sex. When the thought of it gets in our minds and stirs up the hormones, we can get pretty selfish. We let that desire control us instead of controlling *it*, and it quickly turns into all-about-me time.

It's no surprise that the Bible teaches something totally different and something totally better. Romans 12:10 says, "Be devoted to one another in brotherly love. Honor one another above yourselves." Devotion? That's a committed action. Two people are involved, with respect and honor flowing both ways. No room for disrespect or abuse in either direction, only caring about the other person on a respectful, honoring level. Think of it is as if that other person is your physical sister or brother.

Jesus put it this way: "So now I am giving you a new commandment: Love each other. Just as I have loved you, you should love each other" (John 13:34, *NLT*).

Loving others as Jesus would. That's a huge standard, but that's what we're called to do. When you think of that within the context of God's design and timing for sex, it only makes sense. Besides, wouldn't your future spouse love it if, while you're saving sex for marriage, you practiced honoring others as Jesus would? No question.

> *God, I admit it's hard for me to naturally honor someone or love them as Jesus would. It's especially hard when I get off track with my emotions or desires. Help me stay focused on you. Help me learn how to value others the way you do and to value myself as well. Help me grow in self-control and caring for others in ways that build them up.* AMEN.

You, my brothers, were called to be free.
But do not use your freedom to indulge the sinful nature;
rather, serve one another in love.

GALATIANS 5:13

GOING DEEPER

■ Are there ways you've been treated as less than a person of value by significant people in your life? How does that affect the way you allow yourself to be treated in relationships with the opposite sex?

■ Reflect on your ideas about sexual intimacy. When you consider how God wants us to honor ourselves and others, what ways can you change your thinking so that it impacts your choices from now on?

■ Emotions and desires are real and natural, but at the same time some of them can lead down dangerous paths if we choose to follow them. What are ways you can keep emotions in check and honor others?

DEEPER STILL

One way you can honor yourself and others *and* keep your emotions and desires in check is to focus on activities that develop your God-given strengths and that serve others. Over the next few days, make a list of these kinds of activities. Choose one thing from your list and go after it.